S... Poets

Journeys Through Life

Edited by Sarah Marshall

Spotlight Poets

First published in Great Britain in 2004 by
SPOTLIGHT POETS
Remus House
Coltsfoot Drive
Peterborough
PE2 9JX
Telephone: 01733 898102
Fax: 01733 313524
Website: www.forwardpress.co.uk

SB ISBN 1 84077 116 X

Foreword

As a nation of poetry writers and lovers, many of us are still surprisingly reluctant to go out and actually buy the books we cherish so much. Often when searching out the work of newer and less known authors it becomes a near impossible mission to track down the sort of books you require. In an effort to break away from the endless clutter of seemingly unrelated poems from authors we know nothing or little about; Spotlight Poets has opened up a doorway to something quite special.

Journeys Through Life is a collection of poems to be cherished forever; featuring the work of twelve captivating poets each with a selection of their very best work. Placing that alongside their own personal profile gives a complete feel for the way each author works, allowing for a clearer idea of the true feelings and reasoning behind the poems.

The poems and poets have been chosen and presented in a complementary anthology that offers a variety of ideals and ideas, capable of moving the heart, mind and soul of the reader.

Sarah Marshall

Contents

The Authors & Poems

Christine Spall

I was born in London in 1937 and lived a very hard life; by the time I was fifteen I was completely on my own in a bedsit with an engineering job in a factory! Many years later, and many jobs later, I had a wealth of experience to fall back on for my poetry.

I moved to Peterborough in 1961, five children and many more jobs later, life has finally settled down and I have all the time in the world to write my beloved poetry.

I was very suddenly widowed in May of last year. Meningitis claimed my lovely one and I was devastated. My lovely children gave all the support they possibly could and with the help of God I turned back to my poetry for solace.

Over the past three years I have been very lucky in having some of my poetry published in several anthologies, and I've also had a children's book published as well. I will keep on writing my poetry, I am never alone as long as I have a piece of paper and a pencil by my side.

A Sign Of The Times

I look at the newspaper and what do I see?
A battered and bruised face staring back at me,
The question that lurks in those bloodshot eyes,
Is not pity or anger. They just ask 'Why?'
Respect for the elderly I was taught at school,
But the people who do this have no respect at all,
It's the elderly folk who have paved the way,
For the freedom and the life that we have today,
They have earned the right to walk the streets without fear,
Not to be robbed of money or things they hold dear,
The humiliation they suffer is a terrible disgrace,
I hope I never have to see another bruised and battered face!

I Love To Write Poetry

I love to write poetry, it's a way of life
Where I create my very own world
I forget I'm just a housewife
My lines are like strings of pearls.
I can enter the wonder of a child's mind
Seeing the world through their eyes
And make a fairy world unwind,
I can even hear the fairies' sighs
I can see nature in all of its glory
The gardens, woods and streams
Each bush and tree tells its own story
In my garden of dreams
And time goes by as I get carried away,
I've spent so long in writing
Now it's the end of the day
And it's gone as quick as lightning.
I love to write poetry, it's a way of life
But I must show my bungalow
That it's got a good housewife
I'll make the little place glow
But tomorrow is another day
When just for a few hours
I can get carried away
In lovely golden showers
Back into the world I create
I love to write poetry.
For me, it's just great!

After The Rain

The rain has lashed the petals off the wild rose hedge
Now, like drenched confetti, their perfume fills the air
The trees are playing host to the rain, as if in silent pledge,
They display the silver raindrops, a thousand diamonds twinkling there
The rain has been caught on the spiders' webs, giving us flawless
strings of pearls
The grey clouds drift across the sky, changing shape in silent whirls
Little birds flutter in the puddles, nature's bath for our feathered friends
Even a stray cat drinks from one of these, his tail flicks and bends
All kinds of flowers that were wilting, now hold up their heads,
awaiting the sun
Now the grey clouds turn into white cotton wool, for a while their
task is done.
Rain has mixed with oil in the road, giving us a rainbow on the ground.
Children splash in puddles, squealing as they chase each other around.
With grateful eyes I have seen all these wonders, but I know they
won't remain,
For all these things only happen once, until the next shower of rain.

Ode To A Typewriter

I thought that I could type, ha, ha!
But that was before I tried, ha, ha!
For two hours or more I've sat on me bum,
And now the bloody thing's gone numb.
Me fingers hurt and throb like mad,
And to top it all, me typing is bad.
I'm using the end of me fingertip,
Which makes me feel just like a prize dick.
Me dream of a big plush office has gone,
So I'm doing me best with this poem for John.
One thing's for certain, I ain't gonna give in.
Me typing will soon be as neat as a new pin,
Now hear this, bum, I've a cushion for you,
And some ice-cold water for me fingers too.
Practice makes perfect, or so they say,
I'll get the hang of it yet, but not today!

Stars And Fairies

The moonbeam fairy flies at night
Her glittering wings in hovering flight
She sees the golden stars shining there
Gently she picks two and places them in her hair,
Another, she thinks, will look quite pretty
But she drops it, which really is a pity
Silently it falls to the ground
And lands there with hardly a sound
Not to be outdone, some more she picks
But the lovely stars seem to be playing tricks
For these to fall into the grass so green
Making the best display ever to be seen
So now you know how the daisies came
They are upside down stars
From the moon fairy's game.

Trying My Best

A nice new sheet of paper
With lines waiting to be filled
Gleaming, white, stares back at me
While ideas round my head are milled
What poem can I write today?
What subject should I choose?
It seems writer's block has taken over
So I'll just sit here a while and muse
For I know that sooner or later
Many thoughts will come to my head
And I won't be able to write fast enough
Even taking my book to bed
This is nature's way of taking a rest
From the poetry I love to write
And I'll let you into a little secret
All my best poetry is written at night.

Fluffy

I'm white and fluffy and adorable,
At least that's what I'm told,
I didn't mean to tangle your wool,
Mistress, please don't scold.
I'm only a baby Persian
I know I've a lot to learn yet
But was it really necessary
That visit to the vet?
And those lovely little fishes
Swimming round in that tank,
I'd love to jump in and join them,
Tried it once and got a spank!
I love it when Mistress strokes me
And gives me a special treat,
But I'm more interested in that cage,
And the thing that says, 'Tweet, tweet, tweet!'
I suppose that I should behave myself,
For my mistress, I'll try to be good
I'll grow up wise and dignified
Like all good Persians should.

A Breed Apart

You don't have to be a horse lover to stand and admire,
The wonderful sight of that noble beast we all know as the 'shire',
It used to be traditional to see them on farms pulling the plough,
But it takes a special *Shire Horse Show* just to see them now,
They can touch the scales at nearly a ton and stand almost 6ft tall,
I stand next to one and I'm humbled, insignificant and small,
Known as the 'gentle giants', loved for their sheer size and power,
It's a privilege to be amongst them, even for a few hours,
The shire not only loves working, he loves to be ridden too,
Just watch his gentle patience while waiting for his new shoes,
There are thought to be only 3000 shires left in the whole of the UK,
But they still evoke strong feelings amongst the public today,
Australia, Canada and the United States also love this noble steed,
A top stallion at £25,000 will be snapped up with the greatest speed,
But the picture of the typical rural scene puts great pride in my heart,
For I've seen the shire as he used to be, magnificent, a breed apart!

Lost Love

I sit in the room with him, the man who once held my heart,
I watch the sensual lips that told me we'd never part
The familiar eyes that still search mine, reaching into my soul
And how I loved him, my life was complete and whole
I watch his muscular arms that held me gently for so long
And felt once more that feeling, long after he had gone.
The wanting to be near him, the thrill of his slightest touch,
Oh, that loving feeling, to me he meant so much.
But now we are divided, each going our separate ways
And I remember the love we shared, through a misty haze
A misunderstanding, a split decision, I thought that I knew best
Little did I realise that our love would be put to the test,
And even though he visits me, I don't know if he feels the same
For although I search his eyes, all I can see is his pain.
What would I give to see those lips formed into a kiss?
To see in his eyes that loving look that I have sorely missed?
How I regret that fateful day I decided we should part,
Now I'm sitting in the room with him, he who stole my heart.

Nature's Orchestra

We are all motivated by music, be it folk, country or soul,
Some like the classical pieces while others like rock 'n' roll.
I love to hear all of these sounds but the music that motivates me,
Is the beautiful music of nature, rich in its simplicity.
Take the dawn chorus of birds, there's no conductor needed there,
Every note is perfect and sweet as it fills the morning air.
Listen to the grasshoppers rasp and the gentle buzzing of the bee,
These are chords that need no prompting, they can use them instantly.
The crescendo of an angry sea, the ripple of a gentle brook,
All these are musical notes, not to be found in any book.
The sound of thunder and lightning, the beating of rain on the ground,
These are the elements' contribution, to nature's orchestral sounds.

The Seed

A tiny seed is planted in four or five inches of soil,
Instinct tells it that it has to prove its worth.
For weeks and weeks it struggles, fighting through the soil,
And then one day a shoot peeps through, reward for all that toil.
If this plant must reach full growth then man must play his part,
For he must feed and water it with loving care in his heart,
And for that care he will be blessed a hundred times and more
For that plant will bring forth a bloom like he's never seen before
The bloom will flourish, then wither and die, but do not shed a tear,
For the plant has produced another seed, ready for planting next year.

How much like that little plant is the wonderful birth of man?
For he is also born of seed, which we must nourish for as long as we can.
Not only nourishment for the body but also for the mind
So that when he grows he can take his place amongst mankind
Through infancy and adolescence we must teach him of the love,
That we receive and keep on receiving from the Father God above,
For this child to be full grown and reach maturity
With great care we must teach him love and purity
Only then will we know if we have proved our worth
For all the years that we have lived on Father God's treasure Earth.

Silver Birch

The silver birch so slender and tall
Perched on the river's edge
Watching the river's endless flow
What secrets you must know
You stand there on a slender limb
Graceful and so proud
Stretching your cool and leafy head
To the sunlight and the clouds
Oh silver birch, don't ever change
One silver leaf on your bough
For when I gaze at you I see
Nature's beauty endowed in thee.

The Miracle

My eyes have seen the wonder of a kestrel's hovering flight
And I have often marvelled at the keenness of his sight,
For how could it be possible for anything to see
A little mole, a tiny mouse, or maybe even me
From such an incredible staggering height?
Yes, I have seen the wonder of a kestrel's hovering flight.

My eyes have seen the wonder of a squirrel in the trees
Jumping like an acrobat and disappearing in the leaves
Deep inside a hollow tree trunk once I peeped
And there I saw a squirrel deep in winter's sleep
With his little store of nuts and acorns lying all around

I have seen the glory of a butterfly's birth
Shaking a hard chrysalis from its tiny girth
And I waited until the sun dried its delicate wings
And I have gazed in wonder at this tiny little thing,
From such a hard exterior comes a tiny little wonder
With enough colour to put any artist asunder

I have seen the balance of nature, both cruel and kind
And it has helped to ease my sometimes-troubled mind
If we could only live our lives in exactly the same way
There wouldn't be the hardships that we have today.
Yes, life is a miracle, that no one can deny,
And that miracle is here, under God's clear blue sky.

Nature

A little ray of sunshine in a storm,
The beautiful colours of the rainbow,
The babbling of a little brook,
Watching little lambs grow,
This is nature.

The morning dew on a cobweb,
The colours of a damselfly,
Frog spawn floating on the pond,
Swallows flying high,
This is nature.

Winter's silent white blanket,
Covering the land,
The appearance of the snowdrop,
Making such a brave stand,
This is nature.

Rain, sleet, hail or snow,
The changing of the seasons,
Rebirth, new growth, what a show,
This is nature.

A Winter's Tale

A winter's sun that's filled with frost
Makes us dream of summertime, long time lost
A winter's sun going down too soon
Turning day into night and spreading gloom
The garden shows no flowering heads
And the bulbs lie waiting in their wintry beds
The trees no longer stand in leafy glory
And the birds trying to find food tell their own sad story
It seems as though a steely cold hand
Has waved a magic spell right across the land
Spreading a chill that cuts so deep
And sending the countryside fast asleep
But the countryside is wise, it knows what lies ahead
It won't always be asleep beneath a cold bed
The trees will stand once more in their mantles of green
The gardens will fill with splendour, where once nothing has been
The countryside once more will be a colourful story
For this is nature, in all of its glory.

Mariana Zavati Gardner

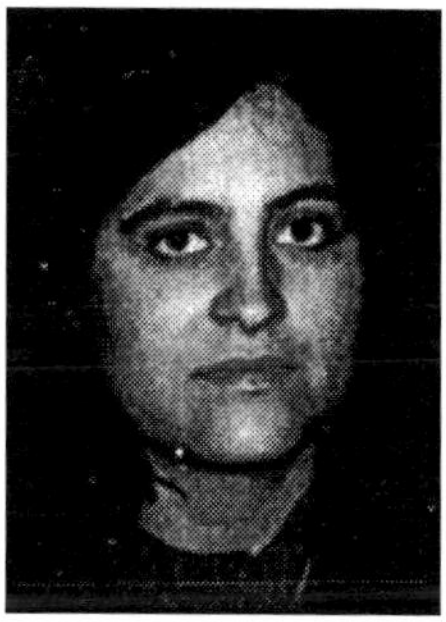

Mariana Zavati Gardner was born in Bacau-Romania on 20th January 1952, the daughter of Artillery Colonel Constantin Zavati, a chemistry teacher and Iulia Bucur Zavati, a pharmacist.

She studied at *Vasile Alecsandri* Boarding College for Girls and passed the Baccalauréat with distinction.

She specialised in languages at *Alexandru Ioan Cuza* University of Iasi and graduated as Master of Science in Philology, double first class honours.

She did a Post Graduate course in Education at the *University of Leeds* and post graduate courses at *Goethe Institut Rosenheim* and *Ecole Normale Superiéure Auxerre*.

She has been teaching English in Iasi and Bacau - Romania and Latin, French, German, Spanish and Italian in high schools in the counties of Essex and Norfolk in England.

She has published various poems in anthologies, nine volumes of poetry, articles on literary criticism and book reviews.

She is a member of *The American Romanian Academy of Arts and Science USA, LiterArt XXI The International Association of Romanian Writers and Artists USA*

She says, 'These poems are images of my experience along a tempestuous time line. This journey has involved shaking off early dreams and facing the storms of ripening age, then sailing gently into the winter of life.

Old fashioned feelings meet our contemporary global world and its serious difficulties.

Dreams like poems must never die!'

The Magical Farrier

My poem is like a kite facing the gales
Dreams of leaves falling in song
The sleep overwhelming in depth
The scent of limes guarding the holy lament

My poem is like dried dew
When waters have finished crying
Mute lips and a song of the mind
The deafness of the comet above

My poem is a dream lying in dust
With no mirror in the empty blue lake
Thoughts of spring burning the holy departed
Seeds of hope chiming a transient dream

My poem is a dying whisper at the fair
Breaking the scent of ripening fruit
The searching day yet to surrender
The Magical Farrier about to descend.

Variations

The maids are weeping on the medieval waters
The song of the merciful is too loud at dusk
The Emperor's ceremonial boat is the timekeeper
Counting the disappearance of the quick sands,
The hunters are sunk with melting eyes
In depth, wolves are biting the celestial lights.

The virginal doe is dowsing on the eve of the Feast Day
The moon is showering the Earth with wounded light
Weeds are laughing in their terrestrial progress
The burdened doe is silenced by the returning storm
Mirrors are crying at the unwanted vigil moving past

Clouds are touching the sky above the fading doe
The flowers of the fungi are drinking from the celestial mist
The hunters have broken the glass of the starched silence
The moon is sifting the absence of noise in the distance
Hurry . . . hurry . . . the paths are melting . . . the paths are moving

The paths are chasing the ill-fated . . . the hunters . . . the doe . . .

A Tunnel In The Clouds

I was digging a tunnel of whispering light
Clouds around seem to touch . . . I feel no flutter
On my wings I cannot rise . . . today I might build
A tunnel of thoughts biting the sky

My dream used to be sharp and bold
It is sad, fragile and small when the day is counted
Measured like the red ibis at the fall of the hunt . . .
Radical men have chairs and desks in the distance

The charm of the cherry tree is alight
Noises of children are in faint blossom
I am building a tunnel of words
To stifle the pending wedded silence

The pendulum might turn into dust
The narrow path from my memory past
Meets at the listening door that is locked;
Faint voices have forgotten the spring

I was the proud builder of a tunnel

Upon The Silence

The Moon is sieving its broken glass above
The silence is deaf and blind in the orchard
I left the keys in the lock of my distant past
I am tunnelling in the clouds to seek absolution

Time is soothing and tender like an embrace
The train has already gone into the storms
When the day has not started to wonder
I am tunnelling in the clouds to seek absolution.

Run in the fog . . . the flowers of the fungi have no tears
The Moon has eaten part of the sky
The Queen of the Night is not tending my orchard
I am tunnelling in the clouds to seek absolution.

The mist is here at dusk . . .
The fungi could drink the flowers of Time
I am tunnelling in the clouds to seek absolution.

A Spring Dance

Young maids are taking
A journey down the waters.
The rustling buds could be
Early sprouting this year.
The fair would open downtown.
The Magical Farrier might gasp
The whispering wheel of fortune.

Galloping mares are telling of
An incensed spring into the distance.
The bath of joy has steamed the windows
Of the approaching train in meditation.
I could hear the trot of the blossom
The scent of the moving bark . . .
The Magical Farrier has transcended.

You Might Arrive

You might arrive and the marshes might open
The putrid fragrant flowers disclosed so sudden
Might remember some fish fading in the direction
Of the shores to mirror their scales in the sands.

You might arrive and the marshes might open
You could disclose the hazy confusion
Some people get when wandering along
The humming path by olive trees and old oleanders

You might arrive and the marshes might open
The vanishing immaculate dreams of yesterday
The hectic today with colourless tears
The scent of the unsure chill of tomorrow

You might arrive and the marshes could be dry
You might just stumble over the backdoor steps
You might break the dreams and the bells would chime
The lament of the holy departed in the hot afternoon.

The Gates Have Closed

The gates have closed so suddenly
The scent of things to come
The bunches set in sizes
The sweat of toiling bones
In parching fields and
The exhausted knitted hours
The clasping hands when
Breaking silent boulders

The scent of ripening quinces
And laughing sunny apples
Stored high above the wardrobe
Each autumn for the winter
The old forgotten storing rooms
The breath of Ember days . . .
The ice-cream seller's lonely tune
Is coming through the open window

Saying Goodbye

The winter is dying with the sunrise
Tears are hanging at wooden eaves
The snowman from the garden is
Just two clumps of coal and
A rotting carrot is peeping from within

The green of the new grass has
Suddenly stifled the glow of the winter
Goodbyes are said beyond the melting horizon
Lovers have made their promises in the deep silence
Winter is trapped . . . its soul is altered for this year

The Bridal Dresser

The breeze has indifferently kissed the blossoms
Some shapes of undetected joy are conceived on the soil
There is opportunity in the air, for the sick and the weak
There is confusion about the way people are made,
How they might rise above the superfluous hours

The waste of so many riches has wounded the soil
They have dressed the ground in substantial grime
Rites of love have fixed a mask of decomposing complexions
I remember the bridal dresser and the garments of
Those precious hours, away from the battling words

Consolation is the key to daily diaries
Difficult to understand by the hard of hearing
The wheat has not ripened yet; in the movable odour,
Meet our errors midway and we shall understand the message
Of the decipherers embracing the light and the dark

I Woke Up

I woke up from an abundant dream
A programmed world of some shape
Not viewed as familiar at first
Someone intrigued showed amongst
Technological forms
It was you, arrived from that original building
Tangled in lime trees and embalmed in scent
Like when foxes are chasing horses or is it
the other way, with young game hiding
In last year's leftovers they displayed
In sight and . . . ignored by true love
Away from the light and the curtains of time
You escaped again behind that expeditionary dream

Follow Me

A gift of love entrances the aromatic grief
A hunger which offends the radiance of the day
A blessing of the night in abrupt ending . . .
Ephemeral equations . . . flamboyant illusions . . .
Follow me to the sands and you will tell . . .
An answer when the farewell voices are at rest
Measured in the confessed fare of the Time Lord
Wheels playing the frustration game
Planets lined to start a new cycle
Follow me where there is silence

The jester moves as the rainbow
Crowns the sky in a half-circle mirage
He tames the hypnotic storms of the soul
In a deceptive ambition to modify the present
Follow me where the dunes measure the Time

Homecoming

Dancers perform at high tide
Chestnuts are in full bloom
Wonder about the scent
And the old hall at noon
Ages are coming and going
Footprints are lost in shadows
Their absence is my memory
Of past times and imaginary returns

Never shared possibilities
Challenged impatience of youth
Expression locked in hands
Time shaped as an abandoned dream
An aunt who stopped the fast train
Cousins who I rarely saw cross
Rivers of trapped recollections
Echoes of promising homecoming.

The Gondolier

On the edge of sleep
Flowing currents
Sighing spasms
In my body . . .
Rattles sifting my soul

Tracing days ahead
Nights tiptoeing to abodes
The gondolier after sunset
Leaves the gondola boat
To hunt freedom in sleep.

My Voice

My voice is trapped within
No fury in the sound to bellow

Running wild like a stream
Nostrils sharp in the scent

Talking hands, reluctant fingers
Roaring eyes soaked in sharp sunlight

Wounding is the fire of those days
Sales counterbalanced in dust

My solar love is asleep
Wrapped in forlorn tentacles

Bridal Musicians

Bridal musicians weave veils
In silent pine forests
Where old Roman roads lie in
Offering, rest and protection

Drums and bridal musicians
Sigh tides of affection
Taste of autumn slowly spreading
Fading joy of cooling feelings
Happy rivers, exhausted and dry.

Blue Paper At The Windows

I remember a mudded stone street
Well-disciplined lined houses
Old people pulling weeds and grass
Growing by the side of the pavement
Little children playing football
In the deserted street when the sun
Is unfolding a burning caress . . .
Houses had blue paper at their windows
To protect the siesta each afternoon
Later on, some vicious rain, merciless
And tropical would wash all for one hour or less
Then people would wake from the deep reverie
And all would move, indulging in chores
Expecting the cool of the night . . .
More and more people would walk
Along the boulevards, until midnight
Would send them home, where windows
Stayed open as long as the following dawn.

Mary May Robertson

Mary Robertson has undertaken two major journeys in life: one as a doctor and one as a patient. She graduated from university and medical school in Cape Town, South Africa, but has spent the majority of her medical career in London.

While a doctor, she has travelled extensively, including being a ship's doctor on a yacht crossing the Atlantic, and then on a square-rigger, which was circumnavigating. She is a Professor of Neuropsychiatry. She is also an international authority on Tourette's Syndrome.

She enjoys opera, tai chi and photography. She writes poetry on specific journeys.

In 2002 she was diagnosed with breast cancer. This has been her latest journey.

The Hug

I was well-dressed in my Professorial attire
I wore my yellow and black jacket
And my good matching jewels.
He was
Tall, dark and handsome.
He was
Empathetic and kind.
The story should have had a happy ending.
He broke the news and told me
I had breast cancer.
I had ductal carcinoma in situ, invasive and stage two.
It was Wednesday, the 27th November 2002.
I told him
I was devastated.
I cried.
We spoke briefly.
He hugged me warmly and
Left me with the nurse.
That night
John and I went out to dinner.
I drank too much.
I was still crying next morning.
My life had changed forever.

Second Chemotherapy

Snow sifted softly
Outside my ward
While chemo crushed the cancer
Inside my breast
Thoughts whirled about, worries, wigs, weariness, weddings
Inside my head
That night I vomited up everything
From my stomach.

Hair

John's hair was black
When I met him
It's now distinguished grey.
My father's hair was a strong wavy brown.
At the end of her life
My mother had no hair
Because of radiotherapy.
My hair is light brown
It once reached my waist and shone
And was always a healthy head of hair
With only three grey hairs
By the age of 54.
On the cancer ward
Hair was a prominent topic of conversation
Most patients had
White hair of
Old age or
No hair or
Thinning hair
Following chemotherapy.
Early January, clumps of my hair came out
I shed a tear.
John said, 'If Mo Mowlam can do it,' so could I
Moulting is revolting.
Friday 10th January, Maria shaved my head bald.

Snow

Snow
Flakes filter like freckles from the firmament
Down into our garden
Which is now
Whitish and freckled.
The Angel on the Wall
Is whiter and is surrounded
By sun, moon and stars.
Snow will now always remind me of my chemo.
Waiting for me tomorrow,
I feel like a lamb led to the
Slaughter.

Ash Wednesday 2003

On Ash Wednesday
We turn our thoughts to
The Holy Land
A suicide bomber
Blew up a bus, killing fifteen
In Haifa.
The weather today
Is milder, grey and overcast
In London.
The penitent pray
And receive the ashes
In church.
Fasting, praying and almsgiving
Should be observed
In Lent.
I will try to observe
And will pray to delete the cancer
In my breast.

Reflections

I had surgery, a quadrancectomy and removing all 17 lymph nodes
From the armpit; the pain was excruciating.
I remember the times I went to our bathroom
To change into my night attire
And I cried and frantically prayed for relief.
I looked in the mirror
It was an awful sight
Myself crying, face crumpled, streams of tears and little hair.
I thought it was remarkable that I looked
Like my mother - but an ugly and almost grotesque version.

My mother lost her hair from radiotherapy for cancer,
A brain tumour which had grown fast and
She died nine months from the onset
Of her symptoms.
She hardly ever cried and was always
Composed, warm and dignified.
I have an album I compiled of her with many photos
When she was ill, with friends, the priest, doctor and Dad
She smiled in most, she was pretty and calm.
I still cry if I look at the album.

I reflect on how I have changed since my diagnosis of cancer
I was the bright all-rounded youngster in a warm family
Then the ambitious, successful doctor, with a man she loved
And since my cancer diagnosis
The scourge has dominated my life - hospitals, doctors,
Physiotherapists, blood-takers, tablets, injections, chemotherapy,
    surgery and radiotherapy.
My mother only received pills and radiotherapy, she died at home.
I think her reflections were focused on the future
She had had a blessed life with health and happiness until the last and
Her eyes reflected the future - in a safe place in eternity.

Aftermath Of 7th Chemotherapy

I am alive
I am not vomiting
I am not in pain
I feel calm
I am warm
I am happy to be alive
I plant for the future.
John and I sat
In the garden
He drinking coffee and me ginger beer, and we were
Welcoming the glorious clematis
Saying farewell to the bluebells
Saying goodbye to the last faded daffodils
Greeting the blue tit and blackbird
Who flew in briefly
To our small sanctuary.

Hampshire Birthday

A single silent snow-white swan
Sailed effortlessly upriver and
Finally joined her mate.

A black duck seemed to struggle
As he followed up the Itchin
Zigzagging across the water.

A bee furiously imbibed from
A purple thistle
I wondered what thistle honey tasted like!

Yellow wild iris flowers faded
In the June twilight
While matching buttercups carpeted the ground.

Birds chirped and twittered in chorus
While sheep grazed quietly
A cow and horse joined in the silent grazing.

John was patiently fly-fishing
And caught a greyling just after six
I almost forgot I had cancer.

The Fairground

My childhood memories of fairgrounds were good
With music and movement and doing all that one could
To have fun with family and friends
Laughing and shouting as we went round the bends.

Cancer introduced a roller coaster to me
Crazy emotions, tiredness, sadness, were all I could see.
The chemo, then surgery, then radio too
After 10 months of treatment what else could I do?

John saved me and took me to a ball
We went on the carousel and rode our horse tall,
We went round and round with joy on my face
Laughing, enjoying and liking the place.

My treatment's almost over, thank God for that.
As my hair grows nicely, I no longer wear a hat.
And with all due course, my body I'll nurture.
As for cancer, I'll dodgem in future!

Colours

Snow sifted silently
Into our garden,
Giving a pure white wonderland
Of soft snowy shapes and
A pure white silk carpet.
I sludged my way to the
Red post box and
Silently slipped in my mail.
Four children with smiles
Jokingly threw shiny snowballs at
Each other, their white smiles
Showing their joy.
A black cab carved
Black lines on the grey slate road
As it splattered past.
At home inside, I sat in our warm
Terracotta living room with
Claret-covered chairs, watching
The snow shimmering and smiling outside.
The world looked like a
Silver-white fairyland today.
It was a far cry from the
Icy-cold red chemotherapy which
Entered my pale tortured body
A year ago.

Tai Chi

Thousands of retirees
Performed tai chi
At dawn in a park in Shanghai.
Slow soft movements
Danced with bright fans
As all moved together in unison.
Monday the third of March 2003
Was the Tibetan New Year and
Jane wore a bright blue and red Chinese coat.
We now perform tai chi
Every Monday
Following the tradition of Master Lam.
Jane teaches us patiently
Movement by movement
We even learn how to walk and how to stand!
Tai chi embraces and soothes body,
Mind and spirit
Without competition.
Our class smiles and greets each other
In communion with Jane, Master Lam
And God knows.

Christmas Day 2003

Christmas Day was very special for me,
With friends and family, and fairly carefree
In addition I was well and alive
A year ago I thought I would not survive.
Over Christmas we had a peaceful time
Six close friends had good food and wine
At the beautiful Country Club
Of some Jo'burg elite it's certainly the hub.
John and I practised our tai chi,
Swimming as well, which could only be
As enjoyable as playing cards
More happy and peaceful than could be measured in yards.
Around the world
Christmas
Was not so peaceful.
The Queen's speech was broadcast from an army barracks.
The frail Pontiff spoke on the 'State of the World' and the scourge of terrorism.
A suicide bomber killed three at a bus stop in Tel Aviv.
An Israeli helicopter killed five in Gaza including an Islamic Jehad leader.
An assassination attempt was made on President Musharraf of Pakistan.
Fourteen were killed near Islamabad.
The Sheraton Hotel in Baghdad, housing Westerners, was attacked.
Sixty people were killed in Benin in a UTA aeroplane which crashed into the Atlantic.
Over two hundred had died in a gas explosion in Chonquing in China.
Britain's Beagle 2 had not landed on Mars as expected.
'We wish you a merry Christmas and a Happy New Year!'

12 To 4 Watch: Bow Watch, South Pacific

Nights spent under Scorpio,
With Antares shining bright,
Twinkling gaily from the heavens
With the phosphorescent light.

Reflecting, too, the myriad
Of dancers here below
In the furrow of the stern
And the bow wave, white as snow.

Dark clouds hung mournfully from
The laughing Milky Way,
Porpoises clad in sequins
Streaked nimbly till break of day.

The squares, the shrouds and heads'ls
Formed the picture's frame,
As I sat in silent vigil -
Until part of nature I became.

Madeline Morris

I am twenty-three years old and live in Nuneaton. I have a four-year-old son who is my pride and joy. We live with my parents in the home I grew up in. I am currently studying for a diploma in 'Adult Nursing' at Coventry University.

Music is my main interest. I listen to rock (new and old), hip-hop, Motown, dance music and ska. I really appreciate all styles of original and unique music and like to go to gigs, dance parties and festivals. I would love to get some of my own material transformed into songs. I also enjoy riding quad bikes with my son, trekking in the local, awe-inspiring beauty spots and reading fiction and non-fiction.

I have always written poetry. In recent years it has been a prominent part of my life. Poetry is a highway of expression to me, it can take me anywhere, at any time. I get inspirations from various sources. Although my poems centre around relationships, observations of the outside world and the culture I have grown up with. A lot of music I listen to influences my writing, as do the people I meet and the places I go. I will get an urge to write, I pick up a pen and then it just flows. I once used poetry as a therapy and a way of defining things that were unclear to me. Now it has become something of a pleasure to me. I like to rhyme, use slang and terminology that my generation use. I hope people who read it can relate to the issues and feelings of my poems.

A Stone And A Hard Place

This dilemma is out of control,
It's tearing up my flimsy soul.
I'm leaving now for a stroll,
To think about filling this gaping hole.
Stuck between a stone and a hard place,
Not meaning to cause disgrace,
I'm losing it, I'm losing face,
Got to get back in and join the race.
The stone is grey and cold,
The place is vast and hard,
I'll have to be bold,
I'm trying and thinking,
Can't put it on hold.
I'm going to climb over the rock,
It's ten past get over it o'clock.
Those who doubted me,
They're in for a shock.

Advice

Take a step in one direction,
Listen, consider, make the connection.
Choose your path and walk it,
Take a language and talk it.
Let your own moods take you,
Don't let your sorrows break you.
Let your own heart lead you,
Let it be your hand to feed you.
Don't ever live a lie,
Or let your dreams just float on by.
Journey to your Promised Land,
Forget the hourglass and the sand.
If you must take that risk,
Your walk outside may be brisk.
Make your own decisions,
Collect and store your own provisions.
Take time out to appreciate,
On your own terms, negotiate.
To exist is a gift in its own right,
Live for the day and for the night.
Peer into the deep ocean,
Realise life is poetry in motion.
Breathe every breath with appreciation,
Don't ever suffer depravation.
Those you love, hold close to your heart,
Then you will know love when you are apart.

A Developing Pattern

Set the pace,
Look at my face.
Go by the book,
Not off the hook.
See down the line,
And take no time.
Read what I think,
Taste what I drink.
Make up your mind,
See what you find.
Watch where it goes,
It ebbs and it flows.
The way that it turns,
Repetition it yearns.
Let it all go,
But don't let it show.
Let it repeat,
With precision so neat.
Accept it with grace,
Vanish without trace.
Let it all merge,
I'm on the verge.
Let it progress,
Without any stress,
Buy me the moon,
I'll be back soon.
When all's said and done,
Let me be the one.

Extra Weight

Too much on my plate,
Bitten off more than I can chew.
My in-tray's getting heavy,
Where's my help from you?
The straw that broke the camel's back,
Eyes bigger than my belly,
Days drift by with lazy content,
Whilst you sit and watch the telly.
Come on, get up, do something,
It's your turn, your time's coming,
Turn it down and listen please,
You're sure to hit the ground running.
I have got both my hands full,
I'm saying this 'cause I'm your friend,
You need to stockpile all you have,
Not knowing what's round the bend.
Whatever happens it is your call,
I can only do so much.
Lady Luck is very busy,
But you could have the Midas touch.

I Quit

I'm abandoning your master plan,
Getting out whilst I can.
Pulling in and cutting my losses,
Handing resignations in to my bosses.
Giving up, throwing in the towel,
Downing hammer, chisel and trowel.

That's it, I quit,
I'm giving it neck,
No plans for the future,
Make decisions on spec.

I'm walking out, I'm leaving here,
Not through boredom or through fear,
I'll be damned if I give you another year,
I mean what I say, I'm being sincere.

I'm not letting you rule my life no more,
Don't worry, I'll show myself the door.
Can't stand this life, it's so mundane,
If I stay here then I'll go insane.
Don't want to follow your regulations,
Don't want your approval or congratulations.

And you know where you can stick my f***ing wages,
I've been wanting to say this for ages.
You're a tosser, a complete egomaniac,
I couldn't give a s**t if you give me the sack.
Goodbye, you w**ker, don't give me your s**t,
I'm walking, I'm leaving, I really quit.

Mental Torment

I'm being bullied,
By my own mind.
I once had vision,
Now I'm blind.
It's ruined this,
Strong irresistible bind.
A love like this,
Is hard to find.

I'm being tormented,
By what I think,
My sanity pen,
Has run out of ink.
I see demons,
Every time I blink.
I definitely have,
A missing link.

I'm a victim,
Of my own dreams,
There's no escape,
Or so it seems.
It may be quiet,
But I hear screams,
I'm hiding from
The searchlight beams.

I will stand up,
And face my darkest fears.
Prepare to battle
Through the years.

Partners-In-Crime

My closest associate,
What's said and done,
Is always appropriate.
You're the man with the master plan,
I'm the girl who'll give it a whirl.
I'm your sidekick,
You're my hero,
Look how far we've come,
We started from zero.
We're peas in a pod,
Partners-in-crime,
For the love of you,
I would do time.
Hatching a plan,
As thick as thieves.
Always something new,
Hidden up our sleeves.
We've made a pact,
We're going the distance,
It's a fact.
For what I'm lacking,
You make up in.
From the deep blue sea,
Arabian nights,
All-inclusive first class flights.
Planning our journey,
Mapping out routes.
In this two-man army,
We're the recruits.
Our mission is simple,
But hard is the graft,
We have our transport,
A bubble-shaped aircraft.
Everything else
Looks after itself.

Precious

You are so bright and full of life,
You ended my needless, material strife.
Emulate light to all you know,
I am privileged to watch you grow.
It's up to me to see you through,
Teach you in all that you do.
I will show you which way's best to go,
You're more perfect than you'll ever know.
To me you are the brightest light,
As I sit and watch you sleep at night,
I thank the gods that you are mine,
That you are fair and you are fine.
You are sacred, you are good,
You're an effervescent glowing flood,
Of love and life and happiness,
You don't have to try hard to impress.
Your heart is good, your soul is pure,
For you there's nothing I wouldn't endure.
I'll protect you with all my strength,
Love like this has no length,
Or weight or measurement.
Just be happy and content,
Then I know I'm doing my job correct,
You'll never know loneliness, I will not neglect.
You are precious, you are divine,
My love for you will not decline.
You will never ever, ever perish,
It's you I've got and who I cherish.

Some Things Others Don't Know

You can see past it all,
Climb over the wall,
Go further, see more,
I have opened the door,
We're packing, we're leaving,
The others are seething.
We'll go further, run faster,
Get what others are after.
There are some things that others don't know.

The bad clouds have lifted,
The gears have been shifted,
You're no longer chained
To he who had reigned.
You're breaking free
And you're coming with me.
The roads are all clear,
And safety is near.
It's not like before,
Because I've found the cure,
It's on the tip of my tongue,
I know I'm not wrong.

See, I know a place,
Where we're safe from disgrace,
We are so near now,
I'll show you how,
You can build a new life,
Without any strife,
There are some things that others don't know.

Spending Time

Can I live on it,
The sum I borrow?
Enough of it
Will numb the sorrow.
To aid healing,
I need a certain amount.
Put it on my tab,
My time account.
You cannot get it
In the sale,
It's valued, it's precious,
It all tells a tale.
Everyone wants it,
It does really sell,
How much you have,
You never can tell.
You can use it,
Just watch the clocks,
It's not in abundance,
It eventually stops.
Your time supply,
Will eventually run dry.
Use it wisely,
Careful how you spend it,
When your clock finally breaks,
You cannot mend it.

You're There

I see you're thinking long and deep,
The morning's here, you're lacking sleep.
We have been through the mill together,
I'll be by your side, leaving you never.

We've been to the brink and now coming back,
I went off the rails, you put me on track.
You give me your love, fill me with health,
I'd share with you, my home and my wealth.

We talk and we cry, we laugh and we shout,
I'm truly blessed to have you about.
You never fail me, what you say is true,
I got where I am, with great help from you.

Alan Zoltie

I was born in Glasgow, Scotland, on January 25th 1959 - *the 200th anniversary of the birth of the great Robert Burns* - just 20 miles from his home.

I left school at 17, and entered the world of commerce. I have run my own company since the tender age of 19. I am an entrepreneur, and I have had involvement in many different ventures in many lands, over the past 25 years. My business now runs several offices all around the world and specialises in sourcing products from China, for companies like Disney and Nike. The organisation and the travelling involved, is responsible for most of the incredible experiences I have enjoyed in my life.

I had never written a single word of poetry until January 26th, 2003. I was on a visit to Half Moon Bay in California and, whilst watching the waves, I felt the sudden impulse to put down in words my overwhelming emotions and it was then I composed my first poem.

I have no idea why this happened; however, my poem *'Half Moon Bay'* was well received by my friends, which both encouraged and inspired me to continue to write about life's experiences.

I enjoy the challenge of life - it is a constant source of inspiration - and not a day passes when one, sometimes two poems, have been written. I have now composed over 400 poems, all of which are based on real-life situations.

My ambition is to create poetry with understandable prose, which everyone can read and enjoy. I aim to paint pictures with my words, depicting scenes from reality and transforming them into a colourful poetic form.

There is not one subject in our wonderful universe that I do not cover. My eyes and mind are forever open to what goes on around me.

Half Moon Bay

So powerful, so tall, so invigorating they fall
One after another after another, it goes on
White at the top and wet in the middle
The foam is so elliptical it memorises, it fascinates

The land has no chance. It is blown into oblivion by the power
One after another after another, they keep coming
A never-ending carnage of water breaking rock
There are no winners, except perhaps those who watch

In the end night falls and like magic it stops
One after another after another, and then they cease
What a spectacle it was, so soothing so inspirational so incredible!
A repeat performance?

Hope

There is hope in all of us
It is all we have
Countless images of where we should be
Likes and dislikes
Do's and don'ts intermingling with ifs and buts
Daydreaming of a perfect future

And then there is reality

My Roots

I have lived and belonged, and then I longed to return
Great distance separated me from my roots
Highlands covered in heather, swamped by torrential rain
Fanatical men in blue and green continually at war
A language unto itself, words indecipherable to most

Front door always open and friendship never closed
Warmth generated by genuine honesty and caring
Provincial lifestyle unknown to those in larger cities
Culture derived from historical circumstance and persecution
National spirit rigid as the stem of our symbolic flower

Shipyards that fed the world with vessels large and small
Changes, making super-fast chips with no pollution or heart disease
Whiskies distilled from the freshest water, life-giving enjoyment
Black gold mined at the bottom of horrendous seas fished by the brave
Ingenuity and invention in an entrepreneurial garden

Castles large and imposing sincere in posture and historical value
A game with sticks creating fanaticism across many borders
The wail of the bagpipes giving inspiration to so many
Place of my birth, the longing in my heart
My upbringing and education
Scotland.

Madrid

Snake weaving across his city
Carrying a hefty burden in his belly
Filled to capacity with common prey
Collecting willing occupants at regular stops
All speechless, consumed by their thoughts

Normal days turn into normal months
Routine, accepted by weekend rewards
Fed by those employed by his master
Faithful in this task he performs
Never questioning the track he runs on

An explosion followed by nine others
Blowing his outer skin into oblivion
Ejecting his food, in pieces, across his path
Utter carnage, killing his future
Destroying the tranquillity he portrayed

Needless obliteration of a peaceful species
Halting the bloodlines of many innocents
Terrorised by unknown predators, cowards
Assassination of the severest magnitude
And for what reason?

Two hundred, gone forever
Starting another normal day, with a catastrophic ending
No longer able to feed the snake
The snake unable to slither to his den
All dead, killed by the hands of the unseen hunter.

Prayer

I was talking with God the other day
Pleasant conversation really
Nothing untoward and no bad language
Regular meetings had become infrequent
My journey in life taking a new direction
He seemed pleased that I had returned
Smiling as we spoke, but really enthralled

My faith had been failing for some time
Like others surrounding me, I was sceptical
Firmly believing in His presence for many years
Captivated by the beauty bestowed in everyday life
Yet He had failed to treat His creation with respect
Parting company and vanishing for thousands of years
Perhaps on a mission in the galaxy to better this attempt.

I was talking to God, one on one
No fear and nothing to hide, certain He would listen
'God,' I uttered with trepidation but also with respect
'What have you become and why am I here?'
He responded with much love and patience
Promising that He had never left any of His flock
Assuring in His care and attention for all who believed

Although faith had dwindled, my hope was genuine
Knowing that His existence was in my very soul
Needing to return to the upbringing I thrived upon
Neglecting these little contra taunts lessened my spirit
Advice from above that was bettered by no single being
Past discrepancies erased in moments through forgiveness
My salvation in His capable hands one more

I was talking to God the other day
My prayers answered with love.

Andrew

His perception on life restricted by his disability
Unlike any normal child, yet somehow more intelligent
Pleasant and charming, he roams his domain alone
Chatting happily to himself, until questioned
Articulating facts and figures from the tip of his tongue
Never a doubt in my mind that they are accurate

His autism making him special amongst clones
Displaying outstanding politeness and willingness to communicate
Lost in his inner self, a barrier of safety from a cruel world
Leaving a lasting impression from the moment we met
Promising never to forget my birth date
Andrew, challenging the rules of normality

Angles

Back at square one
Going round in circles
Plodding the circumference
Rectangular in thought
Obtuse opinions
Too many fingers in the pi

Degree of difficulty
Centred in ability
Angled in the wrong direction
Pointing to straight lines
Going round in circles
Back to square one.

Some Thoughts

Why are we here?
Why do we die?
Why does the sun rise?
Why do birds fly?

Why is green not red?
Why is blue not black?
Why is white so clean?
Why are rainbows rarely seen?

Why do feet always smell?
Why do turtles live in a shell?
Why is the sky blue?
Why do some get flu?

Why is the bible split?
Why were the Beatles a hit?
Why do we burp when we are full?
Why is ice so cool?

Why we think in rhymes?
Why do you read the 'Times'?
Why are mountains so high?
Why is there no book on 'why'?

Rhapsody

Harmonic bliss blowing across fields
Wind gusts creating melodic sounds
Branches catching notes from nature
Orchestrating rhapsodic beauty for all

Tempo increasing pace dramatically
Timpani of raindrops as discreet accompaniment
Thunderous applause from the heavens
Lightning providing perfection in pyrotechnics

Staccato of hail bouncing on rooftops
Noise level raised by two octaves
The clap from the big base drum now overhead
A natural symphony conducted by the maestro

Slowly the performance surrenders into quiet
Exhausted elements gasping for fresh air
Pleasant applause registered by chirping
A steady calm returning to life's theatre

Model

Sleek and slim and wonderful
Put together exquisitely
Beautifully engineered
Flawless

Near perfection and primed
Not a blemish to be found
Superbly finished
Ready for action

Audience waits patiently
All around there is a hush
Anticipation mounting with her presence
Superlatives describe moments like this

Happening so quickly and in one movement
Working with all-round perfection
She lifts off smoothly
My model aircraft, a joy to watch!

Cravings

Cocooned in a case of cocoa
Caressed with caution and care
Craved by chocolate connoisseurs
Creamy creations cradling captivation
Creative designs cavorting inside the cranium
Cool and competitive chefs contend
Concentration on the centres
Cavorting with contagious configurations
Cramming coconuts and cherries
Consistently charming when consumed
Composed concertos of corruption
Candies, the cancer of corpulence!

The Poetry Of Life

Life is so instant
One moment you're thirteen
Then you have kids
Now you await old age

What happened in the middle?
Why so fast?
Life is sometimes a pleasure
The pleasure never lasts

Instant gratification keeps us going
Most of us comfortable in our greed
Passing to others occasionally
Knowledge our greatest asset

Why are we here at all?
The purpose served seems futile
Growing a population of wasters
Uncaring rude and often violent

Should our destiny not be to help
Those around us who struggle
Evolving then at speed
To be a greater species

Time given is but a flash
Making the most of our seventy or so years
Deteriorating the environment seems inevitable
No justice for nature

In time the gods shall win
It may take centuries
Our downward spiral confirmed
Self-destruction inevitable

Too late to stop the train
High-speed journey to oblivion
Our rock may end up barren of life
Poetic justice for the creator

All of the good is being sucked out
Resources will never last
Conservation must be prioritised
Preserving life just a little longer

Chilled

A deathly chill ran through my mind
Onset by complete panic and loss of control
Desire to scream, so intense
Uncontrollable

Thinking too much
Realising the vulnerability in life
Dead end with no way out
Irreversible

Alone and frightened, losing self-control
Needing company immediately
Safety sought in numbers, but from where?
Inconsolable

Talking in the darkness
Assurance sought with one's own words
Age on the right side, perhaps
Hopeful

Finality, incomprehensible
Pulling together the body with the brain
Seeking longevity from above
Spiritual

Calmness at last returning
Abnormal behaviour just a human weakness
Positive attitude assisting survival
Relieved

The Artist And The Poet

His words painting pictures in the mind
Drawings brought to life by imagination
An artist of verbal construction
His canvas in the minds of others

Pictures that paint words on paper
Drawing conclusions from animation
Mastering movement in silence
An illustrator carving life onto blank sheets

Combined they are poetry in motion
Effortless in processing their ideals
So much power in the lines they portray
Enjoyment and education for the consumed reader

Bonded by artistic prowess
The artist and the poet combine to entertain
Each with his own skill and interpretation
Resulting in unique enjoyment with every masterpiece

Keith Edghill

I was born in June 1967 to an English father, Bernard, and an Armenian mother, Hilda, in Hillingdon, Middlesex. Now, however, I live in York, where I am working for the North Yorkshire Police as a crime analyst and completing a history doctorate. I have one sister, Yvonne, who lives and works not far from me, in Pickering. She started writing poetry much later than me, but almost immediately began producing some excellent poems, and a selection of her work was published in an earlier Spotlight Poets anthology, 'Visual Perceptions'.

I write poetry on a variety of themes but the clear majority of my poems focus on romantic love - usually addressing the hopes and fears, love and loss, in my own personal life, but occasionally originating in my imagination. I also write what I might call religious love poems and pieces that reflect the struggles I have sometimes had with my faith. I am now a committed Christian but have only gradually, and with some resistance, started to learn the importance of living my life to serve God rather than anxiously chasing my earthly ambitions, and the full preciousness of loving others unconditionally instead of trying to re-model the world according to my egocentric world view.

My favourite poets include the seventeenth century English minor poets such as Richard Lovelace and Thomas Carew, plus William Wordsworth, Thomas Hardy, and a number of the First World War poets. I share my sister's love of Hardy's poignant and moving 'The Five Students', and am also much affected by his poem 'Afterwards'. I consider the profoundest and finest poem that I have ever encountered, however, to be 'War', written by First World War army chaplain Geoffrey Studdert Kennedy.

Mental Loss

My mind's lost
Like the vanquished frost
On a barren, tundra day
My mind's gone
Like the sun that shone
On the barren, tundra day
For a bitter chill now preys
On that barren, tundra day
Has banished the sun from the day
Has exiled every ray
And order, it has strayed
From that fast and fading day
Stray, stray, mind, stray away.

November

Your dank November expression
Marks no lack of womanhood.
Perhaps you have cried a canal inside
Your moving mascara lochs black look good
The old woman's territory lacks your domain
The new woman's rootlessness lacks your terrain
And all the time that I lack you marks a calendar of dying days.

Five Denier Face

Wearing a smile of sheerest delight
Her five denier face
With twenty-year-old grace
Stretches across the room
Pulls up my spirit from my toes
To the developing pupae
Pulsing choruses in my stomach.

The Girl Who Picks Wildflowers

The girl who picks wildflowers
Sees a flower on a muddy grass verge
Keeping her poise 'mid the road's dirt and noise
She lets all Creation emerge

The girl who picks wildflowers
Breathes in a sweet, honeyed scent
At a time when my heart was dying
I believe that she was Heaven-sent

The girl who picks wildflowers
Will not let her little child die
Before a smokescreen where all that is mean
Kills us one day at a time

The little child who picks wildflowers
Is assured of a mother's love
Dark clouds left and right; dark clouds day and night
But for them a clear sun shines above

To the girl who picks wildflowers
To love and to breathe come alike
With her, winters become an extension of summer
And strength grows again in the weak

The girl who picks wildflowers
Understands me, or, at least, she tries
Sees past the mud to whatever is good in me
Picks out the truth from the lies

The girl who picks wildflowers
Gives me water and light from her heart
But I flirt so with Hell that I choose to rebel
And, well, here I am back at the start

The girl who picks wildflowers
Sees a flower on a muddy grass verge
Keeping her poise 'mid the road's dirt and noise
She lets all Creation emerge.

Mermaid

Your eyes
Hold heavy all of the night and its nightmares
Floating about, flotsam fragments
As you wade in and out,
Trying to be rid of all
But those sweet dreams you know
Just must be there,
Within all the pain, painless, somewhere.
Or are you only happy in your despair?
And won't you let me in?

The Bereavement

In the fortunate life I have so far,
So ungratefully led,
This is my first bereavement.
Mine . . . only mine
For though you are dead to me
With others you are alive.
Though you are deaf to me
You hear others' cries.
Though you are blind to me
You see otherwise.

And perhaps you wish the world
Would burn me or bleed me dry,
Leaving a pound of flesh for the girl
Or a penny for the guy?
But no, you are dead to hatred
And that's what I hate the most:
You rest in peace in your wooden smile
But still I see your ghost.

The Curt Sea

I stand alone on a beach
Alone in mind, even if a thousand bodies are within reach.
I stare away from that beach.
My wind-whipped pupils have only one lesson to teach
That you're of essence to my life.
I'm stranded at sea without you, all lost and alone.
Marry me and be my wife
Or I'll drown in the sorrow I have borrowed and made my own.

You shook the dust to desert me.
Half a chance and you made me incomplete.
Be careful now as you curtsey
Or you'll lose your mind the same place that you found your feet.
Now we are reaching high tide.
Of the thousand no trace; maybe now you'll have space for me.
The storm will calm when you're my bride
For only then will our love flow in harmony.

Separate

You flirted with the fume
As I cried you a seventh glass of tears
A tumbler
Drunk to make you feel humbler.

We took risks
You in your mind, I in reality.
We were self-engrossed
I in my mind, you in reality.

We were self-destructive.
Your lost will and testament
Named me tangentially:
You had nothing to give.

We are separate.
A separation of powers?
But you are powerless.
I'm left holding the flowers.

The Rose And The Honeybee

Proudly parading your pouting petals
Which mark the work of Divinity,
Caught in a snare of nettles,
Sought by the most bumbling honeybee
You ever could see.

I've patience as I pulse the blood of pure expectant ecstasy
But watching you repulse the flood
Of beaux I know are nobler than me,
What hope have I of thee?

If truly you had root as rose
And I'd winged genealogy
I'd fly against nature
By nocturnal nectar cling to thee
Eternally.

Or if you dwelt as now you do,
Sweet fingers fit to swat at me,
The ring of these I'd sting for you
To share a painful memory religiously.

Yet if the human fool were I
Who'd fuel the fragrant flower?
I could but scythe-cut through the scent
Your beauty to devour.

But as it is I play a man
Who wilts as if to die
For you, a lady with a sting in your tale
A story in your eye
Of you and I.

As the golden gleam from your stare
Sees me grow photosynthetically
You cultivate the tremored land of the garden of my dreams of thee
Beautifully.

One day, I pray, your sleeping head
Will dream, due to some memory,
Of a garden and a flower bed,
And you, far from reality,
May fly to me.

Symptom Of A Soul

As nocturnal cocktails drugged the dawn
I scratched at your surface so forlorn
To peel away the pathos from the ecstasy within,
Tear away the tragedy from the comedy of sin,
But I found no smile, only broken skin . . .
The symptom of a soul that's given in.

Lost

I kissed the bliss of known despair
I stared into your eyes
But I found none

Then fell down at your well-shaped breasts
Well-draped lest
My tortoise shell should run

Down further to a misplaced heart
Transplanted in the art
Of meeting men

And if it was not broken
As you hurt before
Be sure that it was then

I looked up to e-bony feet
Beyond this nylon cry
Shone blistered youth

Alike to fleeing leaves of autumn
Reflected in tears
Ruby in hue

And you, with nothing to give up
Gave in instead
A bed gave up the ghost

Of every single misplaced kiss
In places I had found
But you had lost.

Without Season

Even in my dreams you end up with him
Even my dreams I cannot control
Even my dreams my hopes cannot husband
Even my dreams detach from my soul.

Even my heart is a wandering vagrant
Even my heart hangs down to my shoes
Even my heart sobs without season, pumps without purpose,
Beats to a bruise.

Even my mind cannot vanquish the vagueness
Even my mind cannot conjure control
Even my thoughts rhyme without reason, play without purpose,
Gather no goal.

Even my breath frosts my emotions
Even my breath finds me alone
Even as my breath breaks upon the train glass
I'm welcomed by winter with the news that you've gone.

Even my body can't do without you
Even as it begs to do without me
Even my body beads with the June heat
Leaves me my summer rosary.

Spring from my heart, innocent feelings
Fall from my soul, guilt and disease
I have never had a dream of a season
All of my dreams bring seasons to their knees.

Seven Days With April

Our dates were like formal meetings
Your heart wasn't there
Just the silky smile you laddered
Speaking through the chair.
I slowly read the minutes
From the melancholic clock
And when your resignation came, it came as no great shock.

When 'Yes' you'd breathed seven days before,
My heart had leapt the roof,
But my vertigo showed
At the height of my youth.
Your eyes and lips seemed evidence
You truly shared my goal
But the smile that you wear sheer hides a seventy denier soul.

Your eyes that I would die for
Hanging from your face
Your dreams that I would kill for -
In which I had no place
Your lies that I would stand for
That you might give them rest.
I found out when you spoke the truth, I liked your lies the best.

Can I call myself 'Ex-boyfriend'?
Allow me, please, that much -
To fabricate a woman's heart
I never really touched.
I apologise for the seven days
I cast you as my bride.
I'm now wed to my apology - it's always at my side.

The Snow Panther

You have breathed winter back into me
Your whisper is an icy bead of honesty
Your cloak is the grieving mourner's black
To warn that you might stop me in my tracks
With your modesty
Your cold-blooded modesty

Once your stare rendered me frost-bitten
I made to shy from your second sight
But, like the leaf-launched winter cobwebs, you glisten
Beautiful by day and a shining light through tender night

You hit my heart; you miss my smile
You kiss January's merciless ground
But your white heel approaching me up the aisle
Betrays a rose; I buzz with the sound
And July abounds

Now I know the shivering was the premonition
Of your fingers travelling down my spine
Now I see the freezing as the first reason
You gave to me to hold you tight
But I need no reason tonight

Golden-locked, you are my lioness
I cannot bar your way with iron
But your wild lips, red as if with rage,
I shall always cage within mine

Yet, in battle-dress, my beautiful darling,
The panther you greater resemble
As I see, in its silhouette, your soul
Snowdrift-white and humble
What reason need I assemble?

Roy Kimpton

My working years were spent as a mechanical engineer on various large industrial sites. I also spent three years in the Merchant Navy and three years in a fairground as mechanic and manager.

At the age of sixty-two I wrote a community column for a local paper for one year.

At the age of seventy I bought a computer and went to the local college to get my C&Gs in 'Word'. This made me a better writer.

Having been less than academic as a youth, poetry never entered my world until one day visiting the crematorium gardens at Southend on Sea. I said to the lady with me, 'Look at all these nice words about the dearly departed' to which she replied, 'Yes, I wonder where they bury all the bastards?'

'What a wonderful title,' I said. 'I will try to write something about that and 'Where Do They Bury All The Bastards?' was my first piece of verse which Forward Press kindly published previously. Having written about eighty pieces of verse I now only concentrate on song lyrics under an assumed name. The word 'bastard' is meant in its obnoxious meaning only.

Where Do They Bury All The Bastards?

(To a happy divorcee)

As I walked through the burial ground I read one after another,
'Ever loving memory of a devoted wife and mother',
'A devoted father and husband too, now in Heaven but not forgotten'.
Well this made her think of her old man and for the record
He was just plain rotten,
He broke her nose and blacked her eyes and he knew
He shouldn't oughter,
He went to bed with her best friend and then had sex with her daughter.

Where do they bury all the bastards, who give people a life of Hell?
Come home late or not at all and tell you all is well,
Not one stone said, 'He was a pig, I'm pleased he's gone',
Or 'I've waited for this moment for far too long',
'Was always pissed',
'Will not be missed'.

So where do they bury all the bastards, when they are nicely dead?
That my friend is the question that keeps running through my head!

(They must be somewhere!)

The Sparrow

A happy little bird now in decline,
Due to chemical gardening, cats and things of that kind,
Like plastic around the housetops stopping them nest,
It will be a sad day for us all in east or west,
When we no longer see this chirpy little finch,
Losing its habitat inch by inch,
Efficient farming and sterile living might be just wrong
If it robs the world of bird and song,
So do your bit to cherish the wild,
All of you, man, woman and child,
Give them some water and seed,
Or whatever you can for their need,
Provide them with somewhere to live,
The rewards will exceed far more than you give.

Bird Brain

Now I'm only a garden bird, with a brain the size of a pea,
But I don't think we are as daft as the human flock be,
They do things much sillier than we,
They put their bread and food outside, hanging their peanuts
In the trees,
Then they go inside to hide,
We come along and eat it all, just as we please,
When they come into the yard, we fly away with all our might,
They may be daft, but very big and we do not wish to fight,
We often shit on their windows, cars and van,
Some have animals in their nests, called 'dog' and 'cat',
We know all about cats as they kill whatever they can,
Only a fool would keep things like that,
We beat the humans to their worms whenever they start to dig,
Though none of us have seen them eat one yet,
They must eat something good, to make them grow so big,
It must be better than the crap we eat, that's a sure enough bet.

(Well yeah)

The Clone

'Hello, you would not have heard of me,
As I was secretly created and I am a copy of me you see,
My donor body was a vicious dictator,
I've no ambition in that mode, not now or even later,
Being a clone I had no real mother,
Nor a real father or a real brother,
I'm a copy of my former self forsooth,
Far from being a violent dictator, I think I'm a bit of a poof,
My original donor was often told by those he ordered to die,
To take himself forth in his own company to multiply
And that is exactly what he did,
That is how I became his and my own kind,
Will I clone myself again is what you rightly question?
Not bonking likely, what a disgusting bonking suggestion.'

(It will happen)

The Rat

Yeah, all right, that's me, the rat,
The one pursued by man, dog and cat,
We had no choice of what we would be,
Of all the species on Earth to be a rat was my decree,
We scavenge for food and become quite an athlete,
Climbing ropes to board ship to find something to eat,
In warehouse or shop we find a way in,
Where we have our babies and make a home for our kin,
Most humans hate us and cause us to die,
They leave rubbish for us to clean up, so I don't know why,
They kill us with poison, traps and gas as much as they can
So we live in fear of no creature, as much as man,
Some humans love us and keep us as pets,
If we get sick, they take us to the vet's,
They use us for horrid experiments torturing us until dead,
Where did we go wrong? We only wanted to be fed,
They call us vermin but we do not destroy the Earth,
Like they do with bombs, oil, planes, killing each other,
For what it's worth.

(There is more than one kind of rat, rat!)

The Dental Surgeon

'Come on in, lie back in the chair and let's have a little look,
You need a filling here and there and perhaps an X-ray.'
'Ow fook!'
'Sorry did that hurt?'
'Yeah'
'Wash your mouth out, don't spit on the floor,
Go easy on the mouthwash, I haven't got anymore,
My needles are always sharp, they don't come off the shelf,
I sharpen them on an oilstone and I do that myself,
My drills and forceps are nice and clean,
I'm sure they are quite germ-free,
I rinse them in bleach every night
Once again in the morning you see,
When I retire from my profession I will keep my chair,
Then to add a few bob to my pension,
I will use it then to start cutting hair.'

'I don't blame you for that last idea,
As I can't wait to get out of here,
When I came in I wanted one tooth filled,
You pulled out four teeth and I was nearly killed,
I leave you shattered and bleeding and in much pain,
I don't want to see you, you swine, ever again!'

The Doctor

Six A-Levels and now at uni to ponder the path I will take,
My dad was a doctor and he did quite well,
So it's obvious that's the career I will make.
After the traumas of hospital casualty
Where I learned to take loss of arm or leg casually
I then decided to become a GP
Being taken into a large practice group,
My name on the plate and also on my door,
My surgery hours spent repairing patients as in they troop,
With aches and pains, virus and germ, and some just feeling sore,
I've caught colds and flu from some of those I see,
One swine left me with more than one flea,
Sometimes on my rounds the rewards are worth it,
Delivering a baby or curing a bloke with the pox,
When they smile and say, 'Thank you, Doctor,' I've scored a hit,
Yes, it's sad when I have to confine someone to a box,
That's life and we all face the inevitable day,
I could have been a teacher or a collector or rocks,
But I'm a doctor of respect and a doctor I will stay.

'Yes, mine is'

The Politician

(Thinks) 'Yes, alright, I will kiss the rotten baby with a smile and looking pleasant,
When I get in office don't bring your complaints to me, you horrid little peasant,
I will go through the motion of doing my duty to toe the party line,
Keeping an eye out for the odd little cutie, just to pass the time.

If you should come up with a good idea, I will take all the credit,
Smiling broadly for the news, camera and story, you make sure you've read it.

Oh yes, nurses, firemen, ambulance folk and others of similar disposition
Are awarded what we think is proper pay, decided by a special commission,
They don't have to go on strike to get a fair wage, paid for by you and me,
Us politicians never strike, you see,
For every year or two we vote ourselves a huge pay rise, paid for by me and thee.

How dare you call us a load of jerkers?
We don't need advice from you nasty common workers,
You say we make your lives more sad, by doing away with pensions,
Letting criminals out of jail and giving fewer detentions,
If you read about me in the press of the naughty things
I'm supposed to have done,
It's lies, it's false, it's all made up, my wife is standing by me,
She know the truth, it was just a bit of fun!'

('Where did I get the idea for this one?')

The Vandal Cure

'Children should start work from the age of nine,
Like they did in 1840,
Then vandalism would greatly decline.
To stop their games of mischief and being naughty,
If they hate their school, feel bored and will not repent,
For the damage they have done to people's property
Even to their own parent,
Let them start work in the morning early
Not able to go home until six,
That will stop them playing their dirty little tricks.
When I was at school, we had the cane,
Those that got it, never got it again,
So you politicians are playing the fool,
To allow teachers to be in fear of children at school.
Good youngsters want to study and not be disrupted,
By those with minds and morals corrupted,
Who try to look clever in gangs, thinking themselves smart,
Making decent people see them as just another little fart.'

(Any better ideas?)

The Zoo

'Where shall we go on Sunday? I know we will go to the zoo.'
So Sunday came and we piled into our personnel carrier
And as luck would have it, the sun was out too,
When we got there and through the barrier
We bought nuts for the monkeys and parrots that numbered a few,
We saw rhinos, hippos, giraffes, lions, tigers galore,
We fed the parrots and monkeys and other things too,
You can feed them all day and they still want more,
One parrot said, 'F**k off you ugly old git.'
The wife said, 'He can't mean me, I'm sure he means you.'
We endured the smells of urine and shit
'The monkey took our nuts, then showed us his own,
He peed through the cage and got me in the eye,
You should have heard me moan.
So come next Sunday and I do not lie,
You can go where you like but I'm staying home.'

(Yeah)

The Plastic Surgeon

With the money saved up including the fare,
Off to Harley Street, to see a surgeon so rare.
The plastic surgeon looked long and hard at my face
He said, 'Mmmm, there are one or two things not quite in place.'

'What can you do?' I asked anxiously.
'I'm not quite sure, but wait, let me see,
Perhaps the nose can be reshaped or reduced a little
Some work on the eyes, the hair, the chin, I'll soon have you in hospital.
The bone will come from ribs and hips, the flesh from other parts,
Some from your legs, some from your bum but not from the bit that farts,
The scars will not show, if you keep your clothes on,
Your face will look fine,
But will have a different nose on,
Much similar to mine.
At the end of the day, I will have earned my pay,
You will look in the mirror and say, 'Hooray!'

Then if you order it now and you must be quick,
I will make an extension for your tiny . . .'

(Damn, my ink's run out!)

Mac, The Musical Farter

It's definitely beyond folks' belief,
To make good use of your wind relief,
But Mac can play many tunes with his rear,
The full national anthem on just five pints of beer,
On two tins of baked beans and twenty pints in one day,
He will perform his rendition of 'He Did It His Way',
During his act in a theatre, some time in the past,
Some prick lit a cigar, blowing the place up in the ensuing blast.
At the end of the performance he followed through,
The stage manager said, 'You dirty git,
The acrobats are on after you,
And you've shit.'

His musical talent though very fine,
Is now barred from pubs selling beer and wine,
Due to the exit of customers on hand,
Who liked the music but not the stink from the band.
He now has a job more akin to his art,
Entertaining his mates with his eternal fart,
Working at a sewerage farm not far from the store,
Where he buys his beans and beer, to make him fart galore.

(Silly arse)

Horse, Car, Horse

Invented by the Devil to damage the status of the horse,
The first ones were very slow but they are now all fast of course,
This mechanical monster is the essential need,
Of those who prefer it to the love of a trusting steed,
Highly-priced fuel, insurance and tax to pay for,
Road rage, speed fines, accidents and more,
Are the costs we pay for this farcical travel,
To tear around on bitumen roads studded with gravel,
When the car stops moving, there is nowhere to park,
Double lines and a warden searching for victims like a hungry shark,
Garages at home are too small for most cars,
Some become bedrooms, junk rooms or bars,
The fuel for these monsters will soon start to run out,
Then the selfish bad drivers will scream and shout,
The time will come when the horse will return, fuelled by a bag of hay,
The garage will become their stable for the night,
Golf courses will grow their fodder then, well they might.

(What golf without a car? Never!)

A Gentleman Winner

He won a fortune and became very rich,
Money burnt a hole in his pockets,
He had what is known as the spender's itch,
Nice ladies for company and cars that went like rockets,
Charities of his choice were high on the agenda,
Of this kindly man who was indeed a big spender,
Being kind to poorly children and also his friends,
Made the happiness in his life from all his big spends,
Easy-going, nice to all he met, now he is gone,
So has his fortune but not in vain, his name will live on,
When friends and children he helped, live to be old,
They will think of this man and his story will be told,
He liked backing the horses for his hobby and fun,
Sometimes he lost and sometimes he won,
Some would say to gamble your money would make you a sinner,
Not in this man's case, it made him a gentleman winner.

(Inspired by a really kind lottery winner now in Heaven)

Lottery Winners

Some lucky lottery winners are bound to be a bit thick,
Car thieves, vandals, wasters and don't it make you sick?
Were bullies at school and stole other kids' money,
Smashed people's windows thinking it funny,
Broke into houses and did damage beyond belief,
Threw fireworks into shops just for light relief,
Yet after all that above said to have been done,
If they bought a ticket, they are entitled to have won,
So let's hope that the win, if it could,
Makes them more inclined to be good,
Rich man, poor man, good or bad, what is more,
Can buy a ticket and win or lose, that is the law.

(It still pisses you off though, don't it?)

Ninder Raju

I am twenty-two years old, and have just graduated with a psychology degree. I live in a small town called Coventry, which is well-known for its historic sights such as the Godiva and the Cathedral.

Although I am an aspiring songwriter and singer, poetry has by far, been the greatest pleasure of mine for years. Poetry for me is about passion, feelings and emotions, and being able to *live* what you are feeling through your words and expressions. I started writing poetry at a very young age. I have always seen it as my personal type of therapy, especially whilst I was going through hard times in my life, and was finding it difficult to express myself to family and friends. As I've grown older, I have begun to embrace outside concepts influencing my thoughts. We, as humans, are affected by internal as well as external factors, and I hope my poetry has addressed both areas adequately, as both are fundamental in my understanding of life itself.

I feel the recurrent themes within my poems are those of love and freedom. For love is what makes us wish to stay alive, and be truly happy; so lack of it in life can cause major problems. I think there is nothing more special and vital in life then love, in all its forms. The other theme is freedom, be that freedom of speech, action or even freedom to think. Being a British-born Asian is difficult, as I have to embrace both cultures as best I can. What the Western society sees as healthy, the Eastern culture at times does not. So especially the concept of being in love and having freedom is very controversial and significant for myself, and I have expressed these ideas in my poetry.

I would like to thank everyone and everything in life that has inspired me . . . peace.

Love

Within us a passion
Provoked, yet never destroyed,
Restricted and oppressed
But never lost,
Within us a love
So deeply embedded
Contemplation without such would be a crime,
And no matter of circumstances
Or this animosity
This abode will continue
Until the soul ceases to exist . . .

Questions

If the end is never
And the beginning will never be
Set this wildness on fire!
And set this heart free.
If black is white, and green, the enemy
Let the soul remain as it were,
Just let it all be!
So fragments of time, not false but true
Question arose as to who really knew?
Or knows the truth, who's he, who's she?
If reality is a state of mind,
Then set yourself free.

My Sweet Lover

Happiness may be a state of mind,
And joy an illusion of the heart
A flower only materialistically beautiful
A bird only partially free;
Yet my contentment is universal
My love for you eternally true,
Your beauty inconceivably spiritual
And as long as Krishna keeps singing for us
Our souls will remain entwined,
So happy . . . so in love . . . so free.

The Final Act

There will come a time in my life
When my emotions will be at bay,
When insults will never bother me
And I won't care what they say,
There will come a time in my life
When deception above or below
Will seem just a classic movie,
Or just a creative show,
There will come a time in my life
Where life will have neither tint or shade,
And where my heart will be locked
No one will dare to invade.
But in the meantime and just for a while
I will make it through
And maybe crack that beaming smile
But only when it's my cue.

???

If meaning requires understanding,
Yet understanding is without a purpose,
Then that concept was never meant to be,
But exists only in the reality of the illusion.

Simply Be . . .

Barbaric yet confined
Within elements of the mind,
Stiff yet flexible
In a turn of events not yet sure,
Inhumane yet compassionate
Condensed yet elaborate,
Timing yet set adrift
Generosity of greed and a gift,
Not flying higher, yet in a lift
Guilt-free, yet never to shift . . .

Eternal Lovers

What does it matter if the sun does not shine,
When you always shine within me?
What does it matter if the flower does not grow,
When your beauty grows within me?
What does it matter if the world ends,
When our souls are entwined for eternity?

Conspiracy

If colours of the rainbow
Are seen as beautiful
Why can we not find the beauty
In our races?
Anyone daring to speak the truth
Is destroyed
And to wonder,
What propaganda we depict?
Killing our very own concept
Of reality
Who dare say what's there?
When we walk blindfolded
Into the traps
Of what makes our very existence,
Of what makes us simply humans?
Close your eyes
And ears not
Hear the music . . . be free . . .

Will We Ever?

Trapped in darkness
We appear in logic
To be whosoever we please
Yet in sanity
We recoil in humanity
When the mad one
Thinks like a window.

Keep Loving

What is life?
And what is love?
To suffer for happiness
For joy you weep
Roller coaster rides
Heart a fall
To understand impossible?
To keep loving . . . inevitable.

Where To?

Emotions so twisted, making a fuss
A yearning so great, yet so useless,
A life of such wanting, not much receiving
Playing of the mind, words so deceiving,
A moment's thought, and back where I started
Hardships ahead, souls so cold-hearted,
Money so important, yet trivial in the court of Lord
Sins washed away, to bring back you cannot afford,
A walking zombie, if there was ever to be
Blind man standing, not wanting to see,
Packs of lies, tied with a pink ribbon
Wondering where to next, Hell or Heaven?

The Flower

Little girl
Hold the flower,
It is your soul
Your youth
It is your mind,
Your heart
When the winds increase
Do not fear little child
Close your eyes baby
But don't let the flower go . . .

Hurt

Heart is wary,
Promises were lies
Whoever said
Tomorrow never dies?
Saddened and singed
By the truth behind the lie
Please hear not my screams,
As I break down and cry.
Didn't you promise to stay by our side?
What a joke,
That pact you would abide!
Painful to watch loved ones in tears,
Wanting the shadows
To swallow all their fears.
Always happiness
Followed by sadness
Not any goodness
In this house of madness!
Yet I feel your presence,
I know you're there
Makes me at ease to know
Someone cares,
But badness is not over,
For the Devil lurks in corners
Laughing gleefully,
As he listens to the mourners.

Our Existence

If eternity is forever
Then there should be no concept of time,
If love is nothing but an infatuation
Then what of the valentine?
If time is of no essence
Then throw away the dial,
If the water will never come,
Why walk that extra mile?
If Cupid always misses
There's something wrong with his arrow,
Why spread the word of love
When deep down we're really shallow?
If destiny rules our existence
Then why pray for change?
Why pretend we're great philosophers,
When really we're all insane?
If the end and beginning is never,
Then there should never be fear,
Then the question I must ask,
Is why on Earth are we here?

Escape

Trapped
Swallow everything
Do not think
Just follow . . . just follow
Just follow
Await a blessing
That will never come
Do not think . . . just follow
Or break away

Victoria Ruby Collins

I have lived in various parts of Manchester for the whole 23 years of my life with my parents and two brothers until I left home at 17 to live in a youth hostel whilst waiting for my own flat with my dogs. My parents separated not long afterwards.

I left school at 15 because of reasons reflected in my poetry but always enjoyed learning, and so last year I studied for a business administration diploma in which I have done extremely well in and have almost completed.

At one of my primary schools, my teachers, Mr Judge and Mr Jayes found a poem of mine and sent it to a newspaper in which it was printed. I was too young at the time to understand what they were trying to do for me, although I am very grateful and hope to fulfil the potential that they thought they saw in me at such a young age.

I tend to write about my feelings and thoughts towards life and death and the way I see the world in which we live. Also, about my Nana Ruby Harris who died when I was 12 and who was my whole world. They say 'time eases the pain', I believe 'you just get used to the hurting and learn to live with it'.

This time next year I hope to be in a full time job, building on my career and be a budding published author, because learning I had been accepted to be included in an anthology was the best day of my life so far, and I have high hopes for further future happiness by sharing more of my life in the form of poetry.

Worldly Ways

If only we could breathe beneath water and fly to the sun,
Glide above the clouds, see if there is Heaven for everyone.
Reach the end of rainbows, find those pots of gold,
And use it as jewellery, cos favours are currency and money's old.
If babies were always considered gifts to treasure forever,
Past wars were what we learned from, that only ever brought us together.
Only one religion, with commandments of four,
Tolerance, understanding, freedom and love.
Animals murdered, only for food to comfortably survive,
And nudity is not taboo, just something that makes us all feel alive.
Feelings and emotions are something to be shared and explored,
And when someone cries, people don't say, 'It's okay' - because
it's not to be ignored.
Flowers would bloom in every season, time after time,
And snow would fall without sludge - so we don't fall on our hinds!
Could we experiment freely and not die inside of consequence?
For people would not be judgmental, for enduring freedom -
no one would ever take offence.
If everyone could understand exactly what music is . . .
A passageway to your heart, emotions and past memories.
If people took time to love others, instead of wondering how much
they actually liked themselves,
If we judged others on their sincerity, instead of their popularity
or wealth -
We could live life twice to learn from our mistakes,
We'd be twice the fool but for longer - for we'd do them all again.
Mountaintops would be for sitting on and not for climbing up to,
Skies would always be filled with sunshine and white clouds in
constant skies so blue.
We'd keep all things new and dance instead of walking,
You'd say what you are thinking and sing instead of talking.
Would you follow me now, by the mist at my feet
As I lead you into a land, that against it, nothing can compete?
No questions, no compromise - just listen to my words,
And trust in my judgement - even if you think it to be absurd.
Into my heart, travelling into my very soul,
Deep in my mind, surrounding my true spirit and all.
Into the enlightenment of my very self, where this wonderfulness occurs,
It is called progressive thought and imagination . . .
And one day I'll meet you there!

British Culture

Carnival of carcasses; loose souls running free,
Blood dripping from their eyes and mouths - they're terrorising me!
Slaughtered flesh on battered and bruised bone,
But there is no one to care; for I am all alone.
- It's not a crusade, though it feels like a war . . .
I know it's all I've ever known, but what I see, they never saw!
But whether it's a mother, a father, or a baby just born,
A life is a life, and when you slit each throat . . . that life is gone!
Seriously though . . . I cannot even comprehend the thought of dead
    flesh ever eaten,
But killing for 'sport' - well, I'll be damned and beaten . . .
A senseless unacceptable act - committed by an immoral coward unsure,
If he's just completely insane, or an evil freak; through and through
    to the core?
Death and destruction are all that raise their spirits . . .
They see a beautiful creature and their first thought is to kill it!
We should lock them away - but most certainly discard them of their guns,
For what right-minded person would ever kill for fun?

Fire In A Flame, Wetness In The Rain

If you were a bonfire, raging in your glory,
I'd be the enchanting flickering light cast from it,
And we'd be beauty itself - surely?
With people enduring us, with mugs in their hands,
You'd be the hot cocoa, I'd be the roasted marshmallows,
And we'd be the best taste in all the land.

If I were a rose, the most perfectly formed -
With a glisten of dawn's dew,
You'd be its unmistakable scent and the morning freshness
Would contain you.
If you were a smile, I'd make it infectious world-wide,
And if I were the ocean - you'd be the tide.
You can be the first light and I will be day,
I'll be the universe and you'll be deep spaces' infinity all the way.
You'll be time itself and I'll count you till you cease.
I'll be the destruction of all weaponry, if you'll be world-wide peace?
Or more perfectly, you'll be all you've ever been
And never change your ways.
And I'll be all you want from me, forever and always.

Blue Caterpillar Waving A White Flag!

Saddened and crushed, raging frantically confused,
You can't figure out why I'm singing my blues.
You watch me staring into space, but you can't see the pain,
The heartache I've lived with, feel I'm going insane.
Familiar figures flashing violent through my mind. Memories bring on floods of tears,
Thudding like my heartbeat, a constant throbbing through my ears.
Ghosts of my past always dashing my dreams,
Haunting my doomed future, they live within the breeze.
Gliding through my window, the curtain dancing in suspense,
Inhaling deadly vibes, savaging my only faith, hope and innocence.
Tossing and turning, head hung in sorry shame,
Helplessly praying to be spared the burden of watching my spirit grow lame.
Can't anybody hear me? This little lady hunts her shredded reign,
I long to take control of my life as she tumbles to the flame,
I'm being ignited like enchanting witchcraft, she slowly burns at the stake,
For knowing what I know, taking the risks she had to take.
Let her take her final steps now to my times reminisced,
When life was loved . . . now terribly missed.
You don't notice her but she's there, ravaged in a lonesome trance,
Help me laugh and scream the way I used to know . . .
Free that butterfly to flutter and dance!

Perfection's Erection

Let there be life and let there be love,
Let there be hope and let there be trust.
Let life shine and show us the way,
Let us know not of hate, hurt or betray.
Love, shine a light and in darkness bring day,
For all we have is life and love, and let it always be this way.

Tomorrows Never Cease

You're the eye of my storm, my lightning's strike,
My sun, moon and stars, my day and my night.
You're the shimmer on my river, the beat within my heart,
The smile on my face when I hold you in my arms.

I'm your stripper in the kitchen, the maid in your room,
The erection in your hand, the first black rose to bloom.
I'm the invisible tear that rolls down your cheek,
The tingles in your toes that make your legs go weak.

You're the popping cork of the champagne, the highest of highs,
My each and every orgasm, the cherry on the pie.
My good luck and fortune, my future and past,
You are my everything and so something's bound to last!

A Morbid Sense Of Happiness

If waves would lie still in an ocean of tranquil manner,
And I broke up the sky, with a chisel and a hammer,
If I stole the moon and stars, and poured ink in all the snow,
Could it compare to the sadness I feel when you go?

I'd paint black the rainbows and bleed the rivers dry,
Pour the oceans on the sun and leave the whole world to die.
I could burn throughout the mountains, forests and every zoo,
But I'll remain alive still smiling, just as long as I have you.

My Wind On A Wick

I don't want you to light candles to see if I'm about . . .
But when I'm gone and thinking of you - I'll blow your candle out!
Maybe to say a simple 'Hello', or to let you know - I'm watching
you from above,
Or to tell you to stop mourning me because you'll always have my love.
And please don't feel spooked by it, or read too much into my reasons,
Just know that because I've left your sight - I didn't really leave you.
And afterwards when you think of me - because the flame has ceased,
Don't wonder why I came to you . . . but if I blew it out with
my mouth or bum cheeks?

Some Things Will Simply Always Be

Chicken is a dog's enemy, it's every dog's downfall,
Fairies fly missed and statues stand tall.
Walls hold secrets and footsteps sing,
Eyes tell stories and you're everything.
Women are who, they always said, they never wanted to be,
And men will never find, all they feel they need.
Youth is always misused and sadly missed once over,
For nothing's ever missed till it's gone, or in this case
(until you're older).
Blame will always be shifted from place to place,
And people will cut off their nose to spite their face.
You'll never choose a final favourite song,
Glasses always empty quicker as the night grows old.
Regrets are just like resolutions,
And when I mention 'problems' - you'll never think 'solutions'.
The same person will always change the toilet rolls and you'll
forever pick at your nose,
And you'll always know something, that nobody else knows!

Exquisite

I want to be free and fly through life like the breeze,
Just like a butterfly on its only day of life.
In all its glory . . .
Being all it can be.
Only seeing things as being beautiful and new.
Therefore only ever being;
Beautiful and refreshing . . .
To be in the company of,
Not for long though.
Not for nearly long enough.
But being . . .
And living . . .
And seeing . . .
And existing . . .
Exquisitely . . .

Secret Crying Eyes

When the Devil himself has cursed his worst,
A baby is born deaf and blinded from birth.
Never knowing colours, only ever smelling the ocean,
So innocently helpless, in sudden chaos and commotion.
Instinctively turning for their mother, never having seen her face,
Or heard a single word she's spoken, in all their living days!
How do you communicate? What could you possibly dream?
How do you compete to be the person, you feel you should've been?
Naturally wanting children, but fearing the risk they'd be the same?
And you could never really watch them grow, and you may feel
    you caused them pain!
The blind and deaf are special, knowing incredible scents and tastes,
And the spirit within them is almost impossible to be erased.
Touch is extremely immense, especially for their pleasure!
And they can see their sun, when we only see bad weather.
Blind eyes are very attractive in a mysterious kind of way,
Never-ending, deep and empty; like a child lost in play.
I hope it's not only darkness, that lies behind their eyes,
But a creative imagination, and each thought a new 'visual' surprise.

Cold Light Of Day

It's alright to feel pain and heartache once in a while,
But when nothing is learned from the mistakes,
And you keep on hurting more than ever, then you know . . .

Once you can no longer smile at life,
Your sadness just continues to yearn and grow within you.
When your heart sinks ever lower, every day, then you know . . .

You know . . . it's time to let go . . .

To look back on yesterday and feel weak,
Feeling the scales of love have tilted only one way lately,
And it's when they seem stuck that way,
When hope of change has faded . . . then you know . . .

To lose so many tears, weeping through so many sleepless nights,
For your throat to throb through the pressure,
Of trying to hold those tears back, just to get your breath back even.
Your heart hurts, you want to scream . . .
Chasing thoughts round your mind, to where they've previously been.
Then you know . . .

You now . . . it's time.
To kiss your love goodbye.
To tear that arrow from your heart . . .
That once brought butterflies to flutter so gaily.
A final tear in your presence,
A smile, sour - to confirm the painful truth
That there's simply no way back, things could never be the same.
Swollen eyes . . . mind in pieces . . . too many thoughts to comprehend,
Time to cringe and no longer pretend . . .
And now . . . we both know . . .
That this is where it all ends . . .

On The Verge Of World War . . .

Evil showed itself among us, like the world - seemed had never known,
We'd all watched wars from a distance, but now it had really hit home.
Planes full of passengers - helpless - knowing soon they'd die cruel,
unjustified deaths,
Were ordered to call their loved ones, to say all they had left . . .

Headed for thousands of innocents, some jumped from almost
a mile high,
Whilst sometimes holding hands, still . . . alone they died.

The whole world fell in silence. The planet's skin numb,
Unable to comprehend properly, what had just gone on . . .
And for days we watched in horror, as the turn of events unfolded,
Knowing only to well, this was no catastrophe . . . but of sadists -
who controlled it . . .

My Apologies

Sorry seems to be . . .
A sorrow done to thee?
A five letter word?
A tale of time absurd?
Of no going back?
Watching hearts crack?
Seeing tears fall?
Stories not so tall?
Sorry is all anyone can say,
When things have fallen too much their way!
Tears of sorrow, said and done?
Distraught screams thrown from some?
Heartbreaking news? Simple mistakes?
Honest regrets or from liars and fakes.
Sorry, I hurt you. So sorry, now as you cry,
Sorry, I need to show sorrow. Times of sorrowful goodbyes.
Sorry, we couldn't do more?
Sorry, we went too far?
I'm sorry . . .
So sorry . . .
Those words strike straight for the heart.
Sorry seems to be . . .
What it seems to me . . .
Though so commonly heard,
Seems . . . 'sorry' solely is the hardest word!

Terence James Dean (Dixie)

My inspiration for my work is in memory of my son, Christopher, who was knocked down and killed in 1985 aged fifteen years. I started writing verses on the various anniversaries each year, his death, birthday and Christmas; these I had printed in the local paper The Telegraph and Argus in the memoriam section.

I got used to writing notes down whenever they occurred to me and one day whilst having a drink I started putting together my first poem (I would like to say a poet was born but somehow I don't think so!). This was in 1989 and slowly I started submitting my work for various anthologies and competitions. This led to me becoming a subscriber to Forward Press 'Poetry Now' magazine and opened up the world of poetry to me for which I am extremely grateful.

I have submitted work to local competitions (nearest, 'Highly Commended') although I have not yet joined their writers' circle because my other hobby is local amateur football, which takes up most of my spare time. I managed the Queens Hotel team for 15 years, I then became the Liaison Officer for the Sunday Alliance League, and the Insurance Fund Secretary for the Bradford and District FA. So after thirty years in local amateur football I am well-known in this circle and this could be an outlet for some sales.

My ambition from poetry is one day to have my own anthology published, perhaps in conjunction with a charity and dedicated to the memory of my son Christopher, also to have a poem selected for the 'Top 100 Poets' competiton. My poetry, I would like to think, conveys compassion with a Christian attitude; it is (hopefully) in rhyming verse.

I am 63 years old and I have lived with my partner, Jennifer, since 1969, our son Christopher, was killed in 1985. Jennifer had two sons previously, Paul and Gary who have four children between them to whom I am their grandad.

I am always jotting down ideas and notes in my local pub, The Queens Hotel, Thornton Road, and some of the customers like to read my poems. A lot of my inspiration comes on my weekly visit to my son's grave, and one day I feel I shall get everything right and compose a very good poem which will convey all my feelings and sensitivity.

Suffer Little Children

Through man's inhumanity, greed and lies,
Children still die, and we are deaf to their cries.
They die through poverty, hunger, and in the cruelty of war,
The atrocities of man, which by our silence we ignore.

Not for these children a funeral for all to remember,
No hearse or fine coffin, bedecked in floral splendour.
Nor at their passing will thousands mourn,
Perhaps only a stranger, with a sack, to hold skin and bone.

They will need no memorial or remembrance, to acknowledge worldly fame,
Yet we should always remember, that God knows their name.

I Still Remember

My walk so pleasant on this bright spring day,
The daffodil like a guard of honour escorting my way,
My feet tread reverently over this hallowed ground,
Because to show one's respect, requires no sound.

Family, friends, people unknown,
In life so different, now all only bone,
Words of remembrance to old and young,
Poetry unpublished, verses unsung.

I now pass by stones uniform in design,
Standing to attention yet no longer in line,
No words required for their story to tell,
Just name, rank and number, and the date that they fell.

So cometh the hour when my spirit soars free,
Lord, let this place, this moment, be forever me.

Graveside

This field so tranquil yet bursting with life,
Excited birds, daffodils in bloom, showing that spring is rife.
Stones, like pages of history, date life from the womb to the tomb,
Some of longevity, others ended much too soon.

Yet inscriptions in stone do not reveal a person's true worth,
Nor does it lie buried beneath this earth,
It lives in our hearts by the standards they set,
These our treasured memories, which we should never forget.

For if the promise of eternal life, is broken at the hour of death,
Then every memory is as precious, as each living breath.

Cut Off

Unlit the candle is nothing at all,
A plain piece of wax, a Cinderella of the ball,
Yet when with a light it is adorned,
Now its image is totally transformed.

Perhaps to a beacon for all who are lost,
A remembrance to others who have paid life's cost.
Yet for some it is the only light they can afford,
Surely casting a shadow of social discord.

For there are those whose lives, will never be the same,
Lives that have been touched, by the candle's flame.
Because the air that we breathe, is the air that it burns,
Taking lives of children, putting ashes in urns.

Highway Robbery

Loved ones have been killed on hostile foreign shores,
As they fought for freedom, in their countries' wars.
Families asking why, as they wept for their dead,
At this waste of life, and endless bloodshed.

Yet families in peacetime also suffer loss,
On roads which once, were safe to cross.
Corners have been cut, to fuel man's endless need,
As nothing it seems is sacred, in this age of speed.

Life is butchered and countryside laid to waste,
By man's pursuit of speed, or is it more haste?
So have all the sacrifices, been in vain,
And has speed replaced war, in inflicting pain?

Undying Love

Religion and faith, we are given when young,
are left in limbo, when life seems more fun.
(Love dies)

Ageing parents put into care,
gone the childhood love we all used to share.
(Love dies)

The dreams and hopes of our first teenage love,
lay broken and crushed, as they told us it would.
(Love dies)

Love that survives for many years,
can end in a fight, for what's his or hers.
(Love dies)

Yet there are those in faith, who belong and share,
children, who for their parents, still lovingly care.
The young will always follow their heart,
and for others love will be, until death, tears apart.
(Love lives)

Life's Spectrum

We may not have time to stand and stare,
Yet we should always make time, to show that we care.
For those who are broken, or bent with age,
Playing out their final act on life's mortal stage.

The young, the unemployed, or those without hope,
Others, whose only release is an arm full of dope,
The crippled, the handicapped, and those of a different colour,
Let us always remember, they are, each, our brother.

Another Dirty Bomb

Supermarket trolleys abandoned in the street
Where half-eaten takeaways carpet our feet,
Fixtures and fittings dumped in secluded places,
By DIY cowboys with hidden faces.

Blossoms of plastic bags adorning our trees,
A coral of oil and sewage polluting our seas,
Our countryside with its harvest of burnt-out cars
Is there no plastic surgeon to heal all these scars?

It does not seem that long ago when money was tight
Yet our pavements were clean, steps yellow-stoned and white,
Today HP and credit cards, ensuring most have money to spend,
Though can a piece of plastic ever be described as a friend?

So if a dictator has a bomb, why create such a fuss,
When an ecological time bomb ticks away, in each one of us.

Full Time

Tick, tick, tock, goes the clock on the wall,
As it ticks away time so precious to all.
Time which through our life, will be our enemy or friend,
Yet whichever it is, it will still have to end.

So if my epitaph be, 'He watched the clock and let time pass him by',
Then at my passing for me you should cry.
Yet if of me it could be said,
'He loved the living, and remembered the dead,
And on those days when he failed the test,
It did not really matter because he tried his best'.

Then today will not be for sorrow or tears,
Just a celebration of a life, of so many years,
Because this I believed is what life is about,
And although the clock has stopped, time did not run out.

Bradford's Battle

Do we really want to see our city of Bradford bleed
Where burning streets run with rivers of red?
Or do we want to sow a multicultural seed
So there are no places we fear to tread?

Our city surrounded by the beauty of its hills and valleys
Whose history fostered some of the most caring and radical people
Of their time,
Should never again be the scene for extremist rallies,
Because racial harmony should be the hill, we all can climb.

So let us all take hope from the past, and use faith to heal the present
And build the future,
A future where fighting, racism and rioting will cease,
Where all are united, irrespective of race, religion or culture,
So that our city and all its people may harvest the rewards
Of harmony and peace.

Guilty Or Not Guilty

The profile of a murderer so difficult to define
Perhaps a friend of others or even a friend of mine,
Tall, short, rich or poor, those in desperate need
Others for whom crime and violence, become their daily creed.

It may be the reclusive neighbour residing in our street,
Or the plausible stranger, we open the door to greet,
The worshipper offering the hand of peace to stranger and friend,
Or the distraught parent when their partner's love is at an end.

Those who bully, be it in the home, the street, or the class,
The driver whose windscreen is only as clear as the bottom of a glass,
Doctors working in clinics where abortion pays the bills,
Other prescribing euthanasia as the cure for all our ills.

Though perhaps it is only those who seek martyrdom, as they mingle
With the crowd,
Where soon the flesh and bone of innocents, will become their
Blood-splattered shroud.

Electoral Role

The election bandwagon is back in town,
Greeted by smiles, yet many a frown.
The loyal, the certain, also the unsure,
Will now be targeted for the knock on the door.
Characters will be blackened, and promises made,
You do not cultivate a garden, without first using a spade.

Yet is our democracy like sun after cloud,
Or is it empty, like the undertaker's shroud?
Votes are counted in an environment secure,
Though if they really counted, it would mean much more.

Seasons Eternal

Do not grieve for me in early spring,
When bluebells wave with muted ring.
Do not grieve for me on a hot summer day,
Set ablaze by nature, with a floral display.
Do not grieve for me in autumn with its multicoloured hues,
My season of seasons, the one I shall least like to lose.
Do not grieve for me in winter when frost and snow surround,
And spring is only sleeping, deep beneath the ground.
Though remember me in a sombre mood,
If children still die for the want of food,
And when parents lose children into the abyss of death,
Then offer a prayer of comfort, if only under your breath.
Should children ever again suffer the tragedy or atrocity
That was Aberfan and Dunblane,
Then weep for me in sadness, for my soul will hurt with pain.

Bradford's Landscape, Another View

The riots finally erupted, as most feared they would
Streets set on fire, authority drowning in blood.
Two years on, and distrust and fear still our companions on the street,
Propaganda may say different, but not the eyes of those that we meet.

This city where many citizens discreetly move away,
Leaving behind the less fortunate to hope, wait and pray,
Perhaps for a Messiah to raise our city from the dead
Before guns and drugs become rule, whilst authority is abed.

Money is invested in ethnic cultures and creeds,
Whilst indigenous pensioners have to fight for their needs.
Homes for the elderly are closed, too costly to run,
Yet we sponsor carnivals and festivals, in the name of cultural fun.

The capital of culture was a trail we were all encouraged to follow,
Yet our journey proved fruitless and the promises hollow,
Money no object as councillors tried to camouflage the view,
But the cracks were too many and our votes were too few.

Yet many in our city work hard for integration to succeed,
Sowing in our desert their multicultural seed,
Should this flower ever blossom, I doubt it will be black or white,
Perhaps a rainbow of understanding, for to be understood . . .
Is everyone's right!

Skin-Deep

Mirror, mirror, on the wall, do you truly reveal it all?
Or are you just a piece of glass, reflecting images like a shining brass
An inanimate object with no feelings or soul,
Where vanity is God playing the starring role?

But history and yesterday do not deceive,
So how are we so blind in what we perceive?
That haunting look as starving children wait to die,
Mothers so helpless, that only in their hearts do they cry.

So why do we still look to you to reveal beauty and fashion,
When true beauty can be revealed to all, by the giving of love
and compassion?

Chequered Flag

The motorcar is marketed on its acceleration and capacity to thrill,
Yet with no manufacturer's warning, that speed can kill.
So our roads now resemble racetracks where speed is 'king',
With the sounds of the circuits now a familiar ring.

Though today this road is quiet, nobody wanting to race,
And all the traffic is flowing at a very sedate pace,
No blaring horns, or drivers that curse,
Perhaps this is because we are in cortege, as we follow the hearse.

We hold back our emotions as the hurt wells inside,
But the air chokes with grief and sadness and tears no longer hide.
So today for another family, a lifetime of grief has only begun,
This is the price we pay, each time we bury daughter or son.

Parental Grief

In the breeze that caresses my face on a beautiful spring day,
Or on innocent faces of children, happy at play.
In the beauty of the rose, bedecked with pearls of dew,
Or the trees at autumn, with their multicoloured hue.

(Chris lives)

In the atrocity of war when life is made cheap,
Or the ferocity of nature, to make whole nations weep.
In the slaying of children in the haven of their school,
Or those with terminal illness . . . why is life so cruel?

(My son is dead!)

Hail 2000!

Babies butchered in the womb is now commonplace,
Like the aged and the sick, withdrawn from life's race.
Yet others cling to life, until their final breath,
Then why so many doctors and politicians, prescribing death?

Countries are bombed, so their tyrants we can kill,
Yet with only the innocent, and children, the graves we fill.
Bombs from so high, they could come from outer space,
Yet the people giving orders, wear a human face!

Bombs can be like seeds, they may blossom late,
Harvesting life and limb, the innocents' fate.
Then with money and aid, we shall try to make good,
Yet can we ever cleanse hands, that are covered in blood?

The Messenger

The artist breathing life onto canvas or slate,
The poet's inspiration to which we all can relate,
The composer whose music makes the world dance and sing,
Surely such messages we should all strive to bring.

The sniper whose bullet is targeted on whim,
The bomber whose creed blasts life from limb,
Their message we also receive loud and clear,
Atrocity, barbarism, terror and fear!

Still Life

The flowers in the vase are in full bloom,
Their fragrance and beauty brighten the darkest room.
But there are also buds, that have not yet reached their prime,
Harvested by man, before their time,
Their beauty forever to remain unseen,
Fulfilment of nature's role, now an impossible dream,
Perhaps like the child, alive in the womb,
Until the hand of man becomes the hand of doom.

Red Alert

The rising sun silhouettes the clouds
Painting islands of peace in a tranquil sea.
For some it is a masterpiece of nature,
Others see the hand of the deity.

Yet perhaps this red sky only reflects the fires of Hell,
The clouds, only thick choking smoke,
As the forces of evil launch all-out attack
In a desperate gamble, on victory or broke.

My Offering

Words that flow like a mountain stream,
The brush on canvas, that creates a master's dream.
Music that makes the whole world sing,
Or the voice that is carried on angelic wing.
The prayers said with such reverence, they touch God on high
Such fortitude and talent, makes mere mortals sigh.
These gifts belong to others and not to me,
'Though Lord, let my offering be acceptable to thee.'

Delmira Balkwill

I was born 16th September, 1920. I am divorced and living in a warden-controlled flat.

I have one disabled son aged 58 and one married grandson with three young daughters.

I walk with the aid of a Zimmer frame and I am slightly deaf.

I write either short stories or/and poems as they come into my head. In fact, anything that catches my imagination wherever I happen to be.

Peace

As I sit here in the sun,
Pondering how my day has gone,
Peace and quiet all around,
Till at last I hear a sound.
I sit so quiet, pretend to doze
All at once a little nose
So softly touches my idle hand
It is my friend, my little scrap,
My doggy pal sits on my lap.

Resting

I'm sitting in the garden
Where the flowering bushes grow
Roses and some lilac, others I do not know.
On my left a grassy bank
Chairs and tables inviting you,
Stop and rest, oh, take a pew!
On my right a patio. Behind a gazebo new.
In front the view is best of all
Because it has some lilies tall,
Rabbits, pixies, frogs and me,
Watching as the goldfish play
Swirling, twirling in and out
Back and forth and round about.

I Spy

There's a little bird outside my window
I've seen him there before,
So yesterday I watched and waited
To see what he was doing there.
Just when I'd given up all hope
He came along, oh so quick,
The bank of leaves along the wall
Was where he headed for.
All at once the leaves he scattered
He made oh, such a mess!
But must have found his dinner there
Today, he's back for more.

My Visit

I often visit a nearby home, the people there are poorly,
While I'm there I often see their animals and pets.
There is a black pot-bellied pig, three ponies in a field,
Four very lovely peacocks, strutting round about,
Two little dogs, two lovely cats, a pond that's filled with fish.
One day I was visiting and I left a little late
I spied the pot-bellied pig and a pony by the gate.
The pony's head was down, the little pig's was up
I wondered what they talked about
It was so plain to me, they were in conversation
For all the world to see.

The Birds

Wonder why the seagulls have to circle in the sky?
Even when the day is fine they still go flying by.
They circle round, then disappear above the treetops high.
We do not live beside the sea, in fact we're more inland,
Are they trying to tell us, 'Watch out, for a storm'?
Sometimes they are quiet, sometimes they are not, still,
It's good to see them, wet or fine, it matters not.

Thoughts

Someone's cut the grass outside, the daisies are all gone,
It's soft and neat, clean and sweet,
So nice to walk upon.
I liked it as it was before
With daisies pure and white,
Dandelions, with heads of gold
It gave me such delight,
The birds they came along,
To search for likely worms,
I wish they'd left the grass to grow
At least a little longer,
So I can sit and ponder.

Friends

I like to sit upon this box to watch the world go by
Well, not the world exactly, just the people going by,
Some will stop to talk to me, offer me a crumb.
I try to make them understand the reason I have come.
This is such a peaceful place, yet very much goes on,
My friends who come to join me, ask me this and that,
Of course I never mention that stupid ginger cat.
Their gardener comes and keeps it neat
The flowers and trees, they look a treat!
The towering pines so near the sky, waving in the breeze.
Cups of tea and chatter, traffic passing by,
Butterflies and bees, busy all the day, I sing my songs
Because you make me welcome, make me glad
You are the best friends I have had.

Autumn Leaves

The leaves, they tumble past my window
As I sit and watch them fall,
The wind, it chases them around
The heaps are getting tall.
We sweep them up, clear the ground
Each and every day,
But come tomorrow, there they are,
Same as yesterday.

Our Trip

Last night my friend and I decided that
We'd like an evening out,
So got ourselves all smartened up
With transport at the ready.
The first place that we came to didn't look quite right
The second was no better, the third was not our style,
So turned about; travelled on; our haven to discover
But time went on; the evening's gone, so,
Back we went, our evening spent
And put the kettle on!

The Wind

The wind is playing havoc with the roses
The petals fall like confetti at a wedding 'do'
The wind is like a little boy, determined, strong and stubborn too
It's blowing all the washing hanging out to dry
The trees are bending double, the garden chairs awry,
But it does not bother me, you see
'Cause I am warm and safe inside
So blow, oh wind, for all I care!

My Haven

This garden is filled with interesting things
Flowers which smell, others do not, bushes large, bushes small,
Ivy leaves upon each wall, a plant pot here
A rockery there, apple tree a little bare, a fir tree
Rising way up high, nodding to birds which pass by,
A birdbath, and a table or two
A bit of Heaven for me and you!

My Hat

I had a tam-o'-shanter with a bobble on the top
My gran had made it for me to keep my topknot hot,
I wore it in the summer, I wore it in the rain,
One awful day I lost it, they'd pushed it down the drain!

Lulu

I am a little budgie, Lulu is my name
I keep my lady company by playing little games,
We sit and chatter to each other, sometimes she lets me play
I am so very happy here, I'll never fly away.

The Tree

Now that Xmas time is over, the tree looks rather bad
Its branches are quite droopy, it's bare and dry and sad;
Its sister tree is still a'glitter with its bits and bobs and tinsel
But both the fairies seem to know that it is artificial!

Patience

I sit here being patient waiting for my dinner
Everyone is rushing round, no one thinks of me;
I've had my walk, done my rounds, helped them when I could
I haven't been naughty either, no one thinks of me.
I've tried to tell them I am hungry, a drink or even two
Everyone keeps rushing round, no one thinks of me.

The Fishpond

At the bottom of our garden in the quiet of the day
You can sit and watch the goldfish, enjoy them at their play
Playing games, chasing in and out, and to and fro,
Leaving trails of sunshine as they go.

At The Seaside

Today we went to the seaside
The kids, my gran, my better half and me,
We ate and drank, and bathed our feet
Played games, got lost, got tired out, you see,
Visited the shops before they shut
Bangles, brooches, postcards too, hats and mugs
With funny faces on, fish and chips along the strand.
Thank You Lord, for lovely weather
This is the first time we're all together.

Gillian Bence-Jones

I was born in the depression and grew up in the war.

When people ask me why I started writing poetry I answer it's more a question of why I never stopped. Most children write rhymes. Many young people write poetry on the things they feel strongly about. Why didn't I stop writing as most people do? I think perhaps by the time I realised how bad my poetry was, it was getting better which is always encouraging.

I'm married to a writer and we have three children.

I'm a farmer and we are gradually converting to organic farming. If you feed and water the land well it generally grows heavier crops organically.

I'm fond of reading, wild flowers, sailing, history and trees.

For some years we've had a 'poetry party' every month or so. We eat first and then take it in turns to read out our poetry. I think I mostly write about people. I agree with Ezra Pound's point that 'when poetry gets too far from music it atrophies'. Poetry often comes easily to me so I write too much and revise too little.

I'm fond of Anglo-Saxon poetry, in translation, a few medieval poems, Shakespeare, Nashe, Ben Jonson, Donne, Herick, Herbert, Byron, Tennyson, Swinburne, (de la Mare, Thomas, Betjeman, R S Thomas.

When I was young, I could learn poetry very easily so I can still say quite a lot of it by heart.

I think the fact that modern poetry is not very popular is partly the fault of modern poetry which often technically accomplished but very difficult and dull.

Stradivarius In Suffolk

Droning gently a sonorous cello
Follows the jig of the violin
While the pliant piano
Chimes a converging tune.
Beethoven galloping carrying
Borrowing the swaying trio.
Here where I lived till I was four,
Here where the schoolchildren
Leaning forward solemnly listen,
Here where the green tiles
Catch and throw, sound and glisten
Fretting time is groomed and stilled.
The cello, sculpted long ago
By Stradivarius, is christened,
The Comte de Sauveuse,
And has sung since the seventeen twenties.
How often has it throbbed
To Beethoven's pattern?
How often has it sung as it's singing now,
Booming along, gravely, gently,
Gravely, gently without cease
Taking us all to a place of peace?

Twilight

Early in the evening
When owls begin to call
And her husband was leaving,
She saw a meteor fall.

The in-between time. The smell
Of after-rain was strong.
She asked him as the bells
Bounced, 'Will you be long?'

No answer. She saw the patches
Of dim daffodils she'd thinned.
The practice bells threw snatches
Of sound into the wind.

'When will you be back?'
The weird white owl's clever
Wings planed to the black
Through the pink. 'Never.'

He said, I'm going to Jane,'
The whine, then the murmur
Of the car as the pain
Like waves washed over her.

The People Wonder At The Star

I asked, 'Do you remember
Halley's Comet when it came
Last time in nineteen twelve?'
And he answered, 'Oh yes Madam,
Yes. That weren't a washout
Like this time. That stretch
From Ipswich t' Felixstowe,
A great sword of light
Above th' river. You could see
T' read by ut. An' daytime
You could still see that plain.
Some wuz frit; they reckoned
That meant trouble
And they wuz right . . .

Time Change

In Ladywood,
Where once skaters spun
The Blue Danube,
The Household and the Club are one
But the old reality eludes
Our present minds.

About and about
Swung her Ladyship
And the upright butler.
The Squire went a good clip
With the housekeeper. Shouts
Stir the wood.

After the gentry
Went the gardeners,
Grooms, housemaids,
Skirts whisk, skates whir.
The fiddler furiously
Pumped up music.

Now fishermen
Sit under umbrellas,
Still as the lilies:
Dragonflies: the pink stars
Of centaury: now and then
A kingfisher.

The Long Wait

She sits and smiles looking so well;
The dinner party fizzes like champagne.
If you didn't know, you'd never tell.

She's waiting, always waiting for the bell.
Tapping at the window comes the rain.
She sits and smiles looking so well.

Round her wrist a strange device, a spell.
We all talk drinking grape and grain.
If you didn't know you'd never tell.

If it rings it will certainly quell
Our laughter. Pouring again!
She sits and smiles looking so well.

A helicopter would come, its noise would swell.
Candle light, the faces plain.
If you didn't know you'd never tell.

Always the waiting, always the knell,
Needs a heart transplant refrain.
She sits and smiles looking so well
If you didn't know you'd never tell.

Flight

I woke up to flapping; 'curtain' I thought as I lay
But when I looked there was a small bird
On the window. It was the wings I'd heard.
I rose and went across: the brilliant day
Rushed in; long-tailed and slim, its head was grey.
Its waistcoat yellow; picked up it stirred
Within my hands and called, a double word,
Released it sped and soon was far away.

All parents hold a bird within their hand.
Be gentle then, the wings are very frail.
You may have quite forgotten flying though
You soared once. You cannot understand
Their songs; and all too often you will quail
To see the risks they run but let them go.

Lily Pond

You hang in clear as if in air,
Cool, cool; weeds far below
Strewn in mud; clouds far above
Strewn in sky. Soft and high
Grow the walls of the green bowl,
Some stippled with chestnut tassels;
Some silvered with willow quivers.
On lily leaves the blue nymphs gleam.
And in the bowl the cool
Is out of this world but even here
Now and again the chug of a train
Comes and goes, very close.

Old Soldier

Slowly he lurches on his stick
Crippled by a stroke
And sits in his chair
By the door.

He flew from his Ford
Effortless, to open
The door for his Brigadier
After a drive over sand
Fifty miles, two punctures,
Stuck twice, then nothing quenched
His energy.

Sitting in his chair he says
'I miss th' garden cos
I'd always have something on th' go.
Oh well, march on!'

He drove into a dust fountain
From the shell ahead of them
'Close!' said the Brigadier.
Bob fighting the wheel, daren't stop,
Bounced over the ruts and said
'Howd tight! That's what I say
On m'little owd tractor.'

Holocaust Survivors

When they came out of the wood
The cock crowed
And the Judas tree flowered
And the cold hungry years
Were almost done
The Beilski brothers and their own
Resolution had saved them;
And every one of over
A thousand people had a story
To make you cry or cheer.
When they came out of the wood
The villagers knowing what they knew
And seeing Jewish faces
Asked, 'Are you ghosts?'

Our Foreman

We were safe when he was here;
Safer at least in this chancy place
Where always there seems to be more fear
And violence and lack of space.

Safer at least in this chancy place.
He was a mighty wall against the sea
Of violence, drugs and lack of space.
We trusted in his constancy.

He was a mighty wall against the sea.
Tall and erect with wide smile
We trusted in his constancy
Which never failed. A man without guile.

Tall and erect with a wide smile
Keeping things going when we were in trouble.
He never failed: a man without guile.
Cutting the wheat, ploughing the stubble.

Keeping things going when we were in trouble.
Although there seems to be more fear:
Cutting the wheat, ploughing the stubble;
We were safe when he was here.

Long Way To Fall

The brandishing beech is bold
As a mountain and brilliant
As a peridot. I remember
My cousin climbing up and up:
His father craning on the lawn
Advising caution.

The eager boy in the top boughs
Is a sad man. His father
Who feared for him shattered
His son's world and no one
Ever managed to put it
Together again.

High Water

They live under thatch. Oak posts prop up
The eaves. Small windows, cucumber frames
In hay. The house stands above the river.
And they call it Yachtsman's Cottage.

Lap, lap, lullaby. Moon-silver
On crinkled water. A seal
Bucketing down on the tide-rip
Then swimming up to do it again.

A yew at each corner
Of the cottage. Three children,
Two grown. Two dogs and a cat.
The potting shed is a boathouse.

Out in the heat of high summer,
Oar blades circle air and water.
Five swans *woomff* over
Rhythmical wings, straight necks.

He gardens, she teaches English.
One-year fat pups
Lay in the basket. One year
The sea killed half the hedge.

The quiet appearance and withdrawal
Of the tide. The smell of mud,
Night and day, ducks and geese,
Gulls and curlew, always calling.

Relative

Time may be swift,
Time may be fleeting,
Time may just drift
But not at a meeting.

Widely Rude

Wodehouse, P G,
Is very rude
About poetry.
All the same
There is no doubt
He knows a lot
To be rude about.

Spotlight Poets Information

We hope you have enjoyed reading this book - and that you will continue to enjoy it in the coming years.

If you are interested in becoming a Spotlight Poet then drop us a line, or give us a call, and we'll send you a free information pack.

Alternatively if you would like to order further copies of this book or any of our other titles, then please give us a call or visit our website at www.forwardpress.co.uk

Spotlight Poets

Spotlight Poets Information
Remus House
Coltsfoot Drive
Peterborough
PE2 9JX

Telephone: 01733 898102

Email: spotlightpoets@forwardpress.co.uk

NATIONAL GEOGRAPHIC

Volcanoes

Monica Halpern

Contents

On the Scene at Mount St Helens, USA

Sunday Evening, May 18, 1980

I woke up to a beautiful Sunday. It was a bright, sunny day. I looked out of my window. I could see Mount St Helens in the distance. The snowcapped mountain shone in the sun. I could see the deep green forests covering its slopes. Below, a crystal clear lake sparkled.

Then, at 8.32 a.m., I heard a tremendous explosion. I was knocked off my feet. I rushed to the window. The volcano had blown! All I could see was a big cloud of gas, ash and steam. The sky had turned black.

I learned later that the blast was so loud that people 320 kilometres away heard it. The sky was dark up to more than 400 kilometres away.

No one should have been surprised by this blast. Scientists knew it was coming. In March, the mountain began to send out a little steam and ash. Then, a bulge grew on one side of the mountain. The bulge grew bigger and bigger. By mid-May, it looked like a huge blister about to pop.

This isn't the first time that Mount St Helens has exploded. Native Americans who have lived in the Cascade Mountains for a long time call Mount St Helens "Fire Mountain". It has blown up five times in the last 280 years. The last time was in 1857.

▲ **Scientists kept a watchful eye on the bulge growing on the side of Mount St Helens.**

Monday Evening, May 19, 1980

I continued to watch the mountain send out red-hot rock and steaming mud. I saw rocks thrown high into the air. The hot ash and burning rocks melted the snow. I watched a boiling river of mud race down the mountain. It destroyed everything in its path.

Hot winds blew as hard as winds during a tropical cyclone. They knocked down forests. The flattened trees look like matchsticks. Every living thing in the forest is dead.

The air is still thick with dust and ash. I'm wearing a face mask to protect my lungs.

▼This car was buried under the ash that blew from Mount St Helens.

Sunday Evening, May 25, 1980

Another smaller blast took place this morning. The sky was dark with ash and smoke again. The street lights came on in some places.

Grey ash covers everything. People are shovelling it out of the streets. Some towns are using snowploughs to clear the ash away. The land looks like pictures of the moon. Will anything ever grow here again?

▲The towns near Mount St Helens were covered in a cloud of ash and smoke after the eruption.

Chapter 1

What Are Volcanoes?

After seeing Mount St Helens **erupt**, I wanted to learn more about volcanoes. I saw how powerful they were. I saw how much they could destroy. But I wanted to understand what they are and how they form.

A **volcano** is an opening in the Earth out of which melted rock and gases sometimes explode. The word *volcano* refers to the mountain that builds up around this opening. Picture fire gushing out of the top of a mountain. That's what a volcano can look like when it explodes.

Lava gushes from a volcano during a volcanic eruption.

How Volcanoes Form

The Earth is made up of different layers. The thin outer layer is the Earth's **crust**. Below the crust is a hot, thick layer of rock. It's called the **mantle**. Some of the mantle is so hot that its rocks have melted. They have turned into a liquid called **magma**. Below the mantle is the **core**.

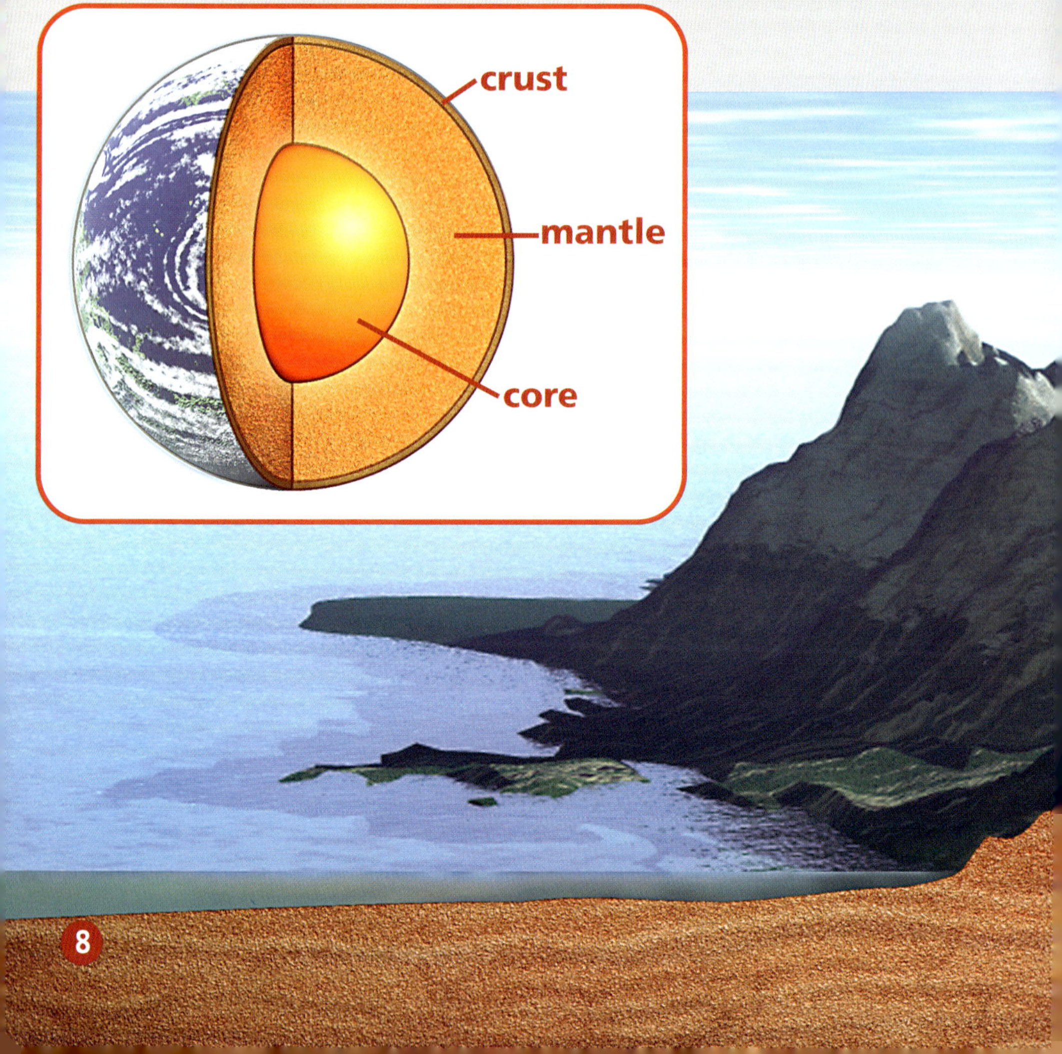

Imagine a steaming, bubbling soup of magma, deep under the surface of Earth. The Earth's crust is not perfectly solid. There are cracks in it. Sometimes, magma bursts through one of these cracks. A volcano is formed. Hot liquid rock, called **lava**, explodes into the air.

Mount St Helens is a volcano that formed long ago. But once a volcano has formed, another eruption is likely to take place there some day.

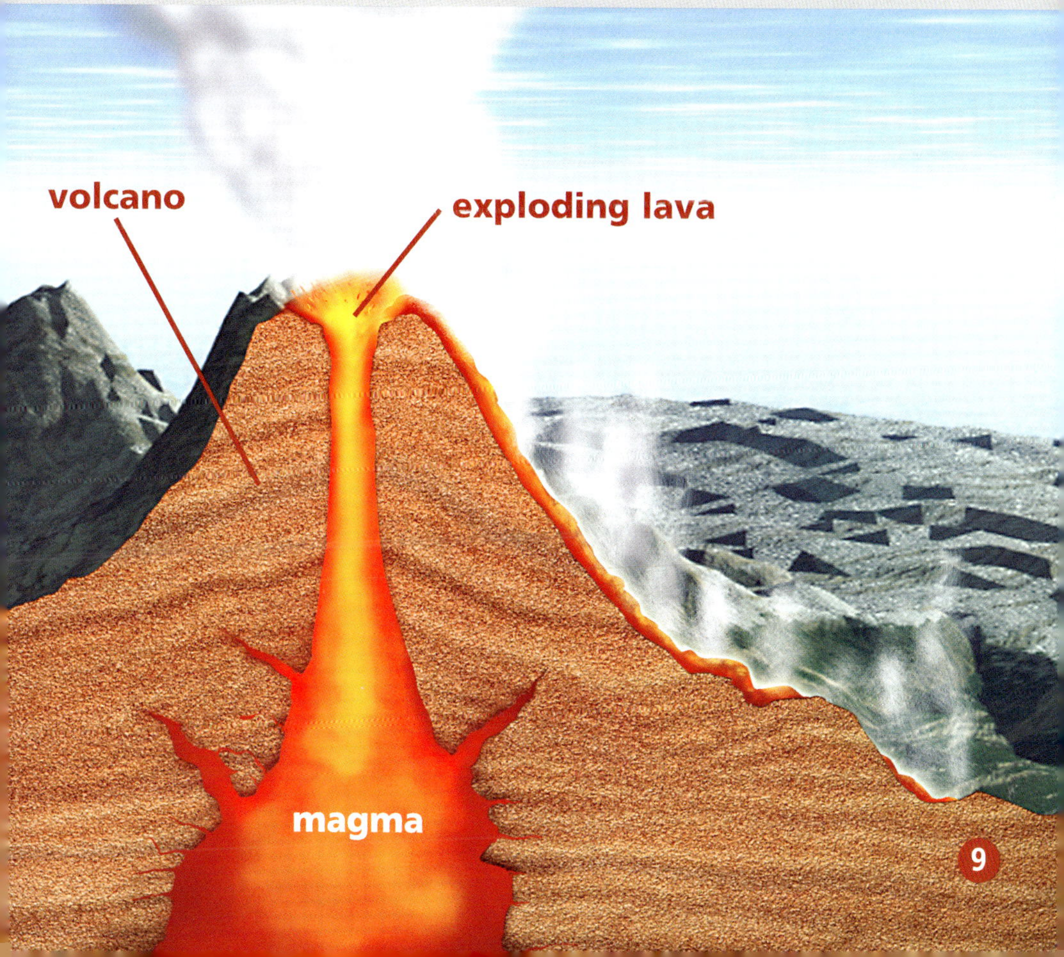

Types of Volcanoes

I thought that all volcanoes looked alike. But I was wrong. It's true that most volcanoes have the shape of a cone. But volcanoes can actually take three different shapes.

A **shield volcano** is wider than it is high. It is large and rounded. A **composite volcano** looks like a tall mountain. Its peak has steep sides. But its sides are often flatter near its base. It's made up of mixed layers of cinders and lava. A **cinder cone** is a cone-shaped hill. It is much smaller than a shield or a composite volcano. But it has very steep sides.

A shield volcano erupts on one of the Galapagos Islands in Ecuador.

I found out that volcanoes erupt in different ways. Like Mount St Helens, some explode violently. They blow out hot rocks and ash at over 480 kilometres per hour! These volcanoes usually have steep sides.

Some volcanoes erupt more gently. They produce a runny lava that oozes out and flows down its side. These volcanoes usually spread out over a wide area. They are low and round.

Mount Fuji, in Japan, is a composite volcano.

This volcano in Hawaii is a cinder cone.

Chapter 2

Where Are Volcanoes Located?

I was curious to find out where else volcanoes have appeared. I found out that some places on Earth have a lot of volcanoes. Other places have none.

Remember, the outer shell of Earth is called the crust. The crust is broken up into big slabs of rock called **plates**. These plates move around very slowly. Sometimes, the plates push together or pull apart. When that happens, magma can move up between the plates, forming a volcano. Most volcanoes happen at the edges of plates.

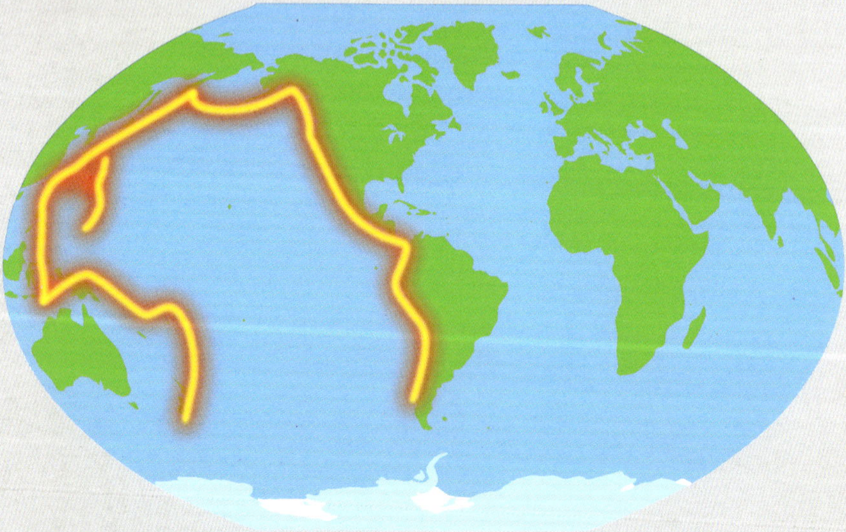

▲Countries along the edge of the Pacific plate are especially likely to have volcanoes. There are so many volcanoes here that the area is called the "Ring of Fire".

Some volcanoes lie far away from the edges of plates. These places are known as "hot spots". Here, the crust of the Earth is very thin. Magma rises up and bursts through the crust. It forms new volcanoes. Some lie under the ocean. But others have burst out of the ocean to form new islands. The Hawaiian Islands were formed this way.

Some volcanoes are quiet for a long time. But they still show signs of life, such as steam rising. Scientists call these volcanoes **dormant**, which means "sleeping". The volcanoes may erupt again in the future.

If a volcano shows no signs of life for a very long time, it is called **extinct**. Scientists believe that it has stopped erupting. There are about 500 active volcanoes in the world. These volcanoes are not extinct. Only 10 to 20 of them erupt each year.

▼Mauna Loa, in Hawaii, is in a hot spot.

People Who Study Volcanoes

I've learned a lot about volcanoes by talking to scientists who study them. They are called **volcanologists**. These scientists watch how volcanoes act. They also study old rocks and hardened layers of ash from eruptions long ago. From these clues, they can figure out how many times a volcano has erupted.

In 1978, two scientists found that Mount St Helens was one of the volcanoes in the United States most likely to erupt. They predicted that the volcano might erupt before the year 2000. They were right! Two years later, Mount St Helens blew up.

Today, scientists are able to predict fairly well when a volcano will erupt. By watching a volcano, they learn to recognise the warnings it gives before erupting. They use several kinds of information to make their predictions. They measure any gases escaping from it. They look for any bulges. They measure the movements of the plates. Small earthquakes near a volcano may mean that an explosion is near.

But no two volcanoes are alike. They act in different ways. A volcano may give many warning signs but never erupt. Other volcanoes erupt without warning.

A volcanologist wears a special suit to study volcanoes up close. The suit protects the volcanologist from the heat.

Chapter 3

Volcanoes in History

Mount St Helens is a famous volcano of today. But it's interesting to find out about volcanoes of long ago.

Mount Vesuvius

Mount Vesuvius erupted in Italy in the year A.D. 79. It completely buried the nearby city of Pompeii in more than 6 metres of ash. As time passed, Pompeii was forgotten.

The ruins of Pompeii were rediscovered in the 1700s. People worked to uncover the town. They found coins, jewels and statues. They even found the remains of meals that were left when the volcano erupted.

The rain of hot ash killed many people. Over time, the bodies decayed, leaving hollow shells of hardened ash. Scientists filled these holes with plaster. Then they chipped the hardened ash away. They were able to see what the people looked like.

Today, you can visit the ruins of Pompeii. It is like a city frozen in time. Pompeii shows how powerful and destructive a volcano can be.

Through this arch, you can see Mount Vesuvius. Today you can still see the position people were in when Vesuvius blew nearly 2,000 years ago.

Krakatau

Mount Vesuvius was only one of the destructive volcanoes of long ago. Another huge disaster was caused by Krakatau. This island volcano in Indonesia blew up in 1883. Some say that the noise of the explosion was the loudest sound in the Earth's history. People as far as 4,800 kilometres away heard the explosion.

The explosion blew the island in half. It also caused enormous waves 37 metres high. No one was living on Krakatau. But the waves crashed onto nearby islands where many people lived. More than 36,000 people were swept away.

Waves from Krakatau spread around the world. They hit the coasts of England and France. They hit North and South America. A dust cloud 80 kilometres high travelled around the world.

Famous Volcanoes

Year	Volcano	Place	Estimated Deaths
79	Vesuvius	Italy	16,000
1586	Kelud	Indonesia	10,000
1669	Etna	Italy	20,000
1792	Unzen	Japan	15,000
1815	Tambora	Indonesia	90,000
1883	Krakatau	Indonesia	36,000
1902	Pelée	Martinique	30,000
1985	Nevada del Ruiz	Colombia	23,000

Anak Krakatau is a
smaller island volcano
that was formed after
one of Krakatau's
explosions.

Chapter 4

After a Volcano Erupts

After seeing the destruction caused by Mount St Helens, I knew volcanoes could be harmful. Volcanoes destroy property. Animals and plants die. People can die, too.

Volcanic eruptions can also change the world's weather. A cloud of ash from an eruption can climb more than 12 kilometres high. Some of this ash can stay in the air for more than two years. It can block the sunlight.

Mount Tambora in Indonesia erupted in 1815. In 1816, spring and summer all over the world were cold. People called it the year without a summer. Crops died and many people went hungry.

Volcanoes can be useful, too. Everything may look grey and lifeless after a volcano has blown. But old lava makes very good soil for farming. The lava has many minerals that are good for plants.

The rocks, lava and other things thrown out by volcanoes have other uses, too. Some are used as building materials. Others are used in cleaning products.

People have found valuable gems and metals around old volcanoes. They have discovered some big diamonds, as well as sapphires and zircons there. Miners have found copper, silver and gold in old volcanoes, too.

New plants grow out of the old lava. ▶

◀ **The village of Pinatubo, in the Philippines, was covered in volcanic ash in 1991.**

Returning to Mount St Helens

Well, I had a big question after I saw Mount St Helens blow up. Would plants and animals ever return to that grey and lifeless place?

I visited the area several years later. I was amazed. Green plants had popped up right in the middle of all the destruction. Flowers were blooming. Insects were buzzing. Birds were singing. Of course, there were no tall trees. It will take many years for the forests to grow back.

Mount St Helens is still an active volcano. Scientists watch it carefully. They think it will blow up again some day. But that day will probably not come for a long time.

New plants and wildlife began to appear at Mount St Helens in the years following the explosion.

Glossary

cinder cone	a type of volcano that looks like a cone-shaped hill
composite volcano	a type of volcano that is made of layers of cinders and lava and looks like a tall mountain with steep sides
core	the thick centre of Earth
crust	the thin outer layer of Earth
dormant	having a time without activity, such as a volcano that is not erupting
erupt	to pour or explode out of an opening
extinct	no longer alive or active, such as a volcano that scientists think will not erupt in the future
lava	hot melted rock on Earth's surface
magma	hot melted rock beneath Earth's crust
mantle	the thick middle layer of Earth between the crust and the core
plates	big slabs of rock that make up Earth's crust
shield volcano	a type of volcano with a rounded shape that is wider than it is high
volcano	an opening in Earth out of which melted rock and gases sometimes erupt
volcanologists	scientists who study volcanoes

Index